THE POVERTY BROKERS
The IMF and Latin America

Latin America Bureau
Research and action on Latin America

For condition

First published in Great Britain in 1983 by

Latin America Bureau (Research and Action) Ltd
1 Amwell Street
London EC1R 1UL

Edited by Martin Honeywell
Design by Jan Brown Designs
Cover Photo by Abel Lagos
Typeset, printed and bound by Russell Press Ltd., Nottingham

Contents

Contributors

E.A. Brett is a lecturer in Political Science at the University of Sussex.

Robert Carty is a Canadian journalist and broadcaster and an associate of the Toronto-based Latin American Working Group (LAWG).

R. Andrew Nickson is a lecturer in Development Economics at the University of Birmingham.

Winston James is a researcher on Caribbean affairs, working at Goldsmiths' College, University of London.

Martin Honeywell is a member of staff of the Latin America Bureau.

James Painter is an associate member of staff of the Latin America Bureau.

Glossary of Terms

ARUSHA INITIATIVE A South-North conference was held in Arusha, Tanzania in July 1980 to discuss the international monetary system. Delegates from twenty countries, mostly Less Developed Countries (LDSs), concluded that the IMF had lost its legitimacy and called for its replacement by a new world monetary order.

BANK FOR INTERNATIONAL SETTLEMENTS Based in Basle, Switzerland, the BIS is the bank through which *Central Banks* settle their accounts with each other. It also arranges currency swaps between its members. During the debt crisis it made short-term bridging loans to heavily indebted nations. It is the forum for the monthly meeting of the central bankers of the *Group of 10*.

BRANDT COMMISSION The Commission consists of eighteen full members, drawn from both industrialised countries and LDCs, and is named after the ex-chancellor of West Germany, Willy Brandt. Their first report entitled 'North-South: A Programme for Survival' was published in 1980, and was presented to the then UN Secretary-General, Kurt Waldheim. The report aroused wide interest, but had little practical impact. Their second report entitled 'Common Crisis, North-South: Co-operation for World Recovery' was published in 1983.

BRETTON WOODS An international conference was held at Bretton Woods, New Hampshire in the USA in July 1944 to discuss proposals for a more regulated international monetary system. The agreement resulting from the conference led to the establishment of the IMF and the *World Bank*.

CENTRAL BANKS Virtually all countries have a Central Bank which the government controls in order to regulate the monetary system. Examples are the Bank of England and the Federal Reserve Bank of the USA. Central Banks control the issue of notes, conduct transfers of money with other Central Banks, lead the interest rate structure and accept deposits or make loans to *commercial banks*.

COMMERCIAL or PRIVATE BANKS They are also known as member banks in the US and credit banks in Western Europe. These are privately owned banks (owned by their shareholders) which operate current accounts, receive deposits and make loans (including loans to LDCs) with the explicit purpose of maximising their profits. They are to be distinguished from *Central Banks, the World Bank* and *Regional Development Banks* which are not owned by private shareholders nor motivated by profit maximisation. Commercial or private banks with total loans of less than US$5 billion have become known in the context of the debt crisis as 'regional banks'.

CREDIT TRANCHES The normal method of drawing on the resources of the IMF is through access to the tranches or 'slices' of credit. The first of these is the reserve tranche and amounts to 25 per cent of the member's *quota*. The next tranche, namely the first credit tranche (an extra 25 per cent of the value of the *quota*) is subject to low conditionality, while the three upper credit tranches (each worth another 25 per cent of the member's *quota*) are subject to full conditionality and an IMF-stabilisation programme.

CREDIT FACILITIES A number of credit facilities are open to IMF member countries in addition to the *credit tranches*. The most commonly used are: the **Compensatory Financing Facility,** which was set up in 1963 to assist balance of payments losses as a result of short-term declines in the prices of particular raw materials; the **Buffer Stock Facility,** which was established in 1969 to help finance members' contributions to buffer stocks within international commodity agreements; the **Extended Fund Facility,** which was set up in 1974 to provide balance of payments support for longer periods and in greater amounts than under the *credit tranches,* and the **Supplementary Financing Facility,** the most recent addition, which is intended to supplement the *credit tranches* and the Extended Fund Facility. The facilities vary in the amount of credit available, the conditions applied and the period of repayment.

EXECUTIVE BOARD OF THE IMF The Executive Board of the IMF consists of 22 Executive Directors, of whom six are appointed (USA, France, UK, West Germany, Japan and Saudi Arabia), and fifteen are elected by country groupings. China is a permanent member.

GATT The General Agreement on Tariffs and Trade. An international organisation operating since 1948, committed to the expansion of multilateral trade, by encouraging countries to reduce barriers to free trade. Over 80 countries are signatories.

GENERAL AGREEMENT TO BORROW (GAB) Originally an agreement between the *Group of Ten* industrialised countries in the IMF to make funds available for each other's use in balance of payments crises. GAB was expanded for the benefit of LDCs after the 1982 debt crisis.

GROUP OF FIVE The five Western permanent members of the *IMF Executive Board* (USA, France, UK, West Germany and Japan).

GROUP OF TEN Ten industrialised countries belonging to the IMF (USA, UK, West Germany, France, Japan, Canada, Italy, the Netherlands, Belgium and Sweden). The Group of Ten continues to function as a caucus for its members and as a mechanism for negotiation among them prior to presenting their position to the rest of the IMF membership.

GROUP OF 24 The LDC counterpart to the *Group of Ten,* though nowhere near it in strength or effectiveness. The *Group of 24* arose out of the *Group of 77* in 1971, and has a mandate to review the international monetary situation from an LDC position and recommend co-ordinated *Group of 77* positions on monetary issues.

GROUP OF 77 The name used to refer to LDCs acting together at meetings of UNCTAD and other United Nations fora. Membership has now risen to 115 countries.

INTERNATIONAL BANK FOR RECONSTRUCTION AND DEVELOPMENT See **WORLD BANK**

IDA International Development Agency. An institution affiliated to the *World Bank,* which gives long-term loans at little or no interest for projects in LDCs, and those areas of middle income countries (MICs) which have a low income *per capita.*

LDCs Less Developed Countries. To take account of the enormous variations in levels of economic development and resources, LDCs are often divided into (i) oil-exporting countries; (ii) newly industrialised countries (NICs), which have become exporters of manufactured goods; (iii) middle income countries (MICs); and (iv) low income countries. Only Venezuela and Ecuador (as members of OPEC) are classified as oil-exporting countries, although Mexico and Trinidad and Tobago are also net oil-exporters. Argentina, Brazil and Mexico are usually classified as NICs, while Haiti is a low income country having a *per capita* income of less than US$300 pa in 1979.

PARIS CLUB An informal gathering of creditor nations who meet to discuss *rescheduling* requests from debtor nations of the loans outstanding to official agencies and governments (but not *commercial bank* debt).

QUOTAS Each member country of the IMF is required to subscribe a quota which is paid 25 per cent in hard currencies or SDRs (pre-1976 in gold) and 75 per cent in the member's own currency. Quotas are determined by each country's GNP and volume of international trade. Borrowing ability and voting rights are determined by the size of quota contributions.

SDRs Special Drawing Rights were created in July 1969 as a form of international reserve asset to replace the dollar as the Fund's official unit of account. They are allocated to members as a supplement to other reserves and they function as credits in the member countries' accounts with the IMF, which can be used to buy hard currencies from the IMF in times of debt or balance of payments problems. Members may also use SDRs in a variety of transactions by agreement with each other. Members pay interest to the Fund on the balance of their holding below their allocation, and receive interest when their holding is above their allocation. Until 1971 the value of the SDR was equivalent to one dollar, but it is now fixed in relation to five currencies (the US dollar, the French franc, the Deutschmark, the pound sterling and the Japanese yen) to make their value independent of the fluctuations in the value of the dollar. In mid-1980 the total value of SDRs allocated was US$22.5 billion.

UNCTAD United Nations Conference on Trade and Development began in 1964 in response to the LDCs' growing concern over the obstacles to bridging the gap in living standards between themselves and developed countries. UNCTAD now meets every four years and acts as a forum for discussion. It is used by LDCs to exert pressure to change the present world economic order.

WORLD BANK Officially known as the International Bank for Reconstruction and Development. The World Bank was set up at the *Bretton Woods* Conference in July 1944 at the same time as the IMF. The role of the Bank is primarily to encourage capital investment for development projects in LDCs, either by channelling the necessary private funds or, more usually, by making loans from its own resources. It has traditionally concerned itself with longer term development programmes, especially in infrastructure and agriculture. The World Bank also plays a central role in development policy discussions and helps to co-ordinate aid policy among donor countries.

THE VOCABULARY OF THE DEBT CRISIS

DEBT SERVICE The amount of interest and principal repayments on outstanding debts that have to be met annually.

DEBT SERVICE RATIO The ratio of debt repayments to a country's export of goods and services or Gross National Product (GNP).

DEFAULT A failure to meet debt obligations, i.e. when a borrower cannot maintain repayments on outstanding debt. A default occurs if a debtor country repudiates its debts or a creditor takes legal action over arrears in payment. More loosely defined, it can refer to any arrears on *debt servicing,* and particularly to any failure in interest payments.

EQUITY RESERVES Banks are owned by their shareholders, not their depositors. Bank shareholders' capital or equity provides banks with a reserve against losses, which is available to repay depositors, should loans be impossible to collect.

INTERBANK MARKET The system by which private banks borrow from, or lend to, other private banks; in effect, the 'wholesale' market for money.

LIBOR London Interbank Offered Rate. The rate of interest at which money is traded between the private banks in the international money market. Loans tied to the LIBOR rate are usually revised every three months.

LONG- AND MEDIUM-TERM DEBT Debt due to be repaid over a period of more than one year.

MATURITY PERIOD The time the borrower has to repay a loan.

RE-NEGOTIATION/RE-STRUCTURING/RE-FINANCING Terms used loosely to describe the efforts of debtors to change the composition of their *short-term* debts, usually obtaining long-term loans in exchange. Unlike *re-scheduling,* this does not necessarily occur when debtors default.

RESCHEDULING An agreement between debtors and creditors to re-arrange debt repayments to give a longer period of repayment for a loan after a debtor has *defaulted.* For private, and most public creditors, the agreement invariably involves delays in principal repayment, but only on very rare occasions delays in interest payments.

ROLL OVER Used loosely to refer to the replacement of a maturing *short-term* loan with a new loan. More tightly defined, it refers to an agreement between borrower and lender to have the option to repay or extend a loan, at specified intervals, under the terms of the original loan agreement.

SHORT-TERM DEBT Debt due to be paid within one year.

SPREAD The difference between LIBOR and the actual interest rate on a loan paid by the borrower.

1 The World Debt Crisis

'Never in history have so many countries owed so much money
with so little promise of repayment.'

Time, **January 1983**

In August 1982, Mexico announced that it could no longer meet the
repayment obligations on its US$80 billion* of international debt. The
effect of this declaration — 'like an atom bomb being dropped on the
world financial system', according to one US bank official — was
compounded shortly after when both Brazil and Argentina made
similar announcements. These three Latin American countries
together owe US$200 billion to foreign governments, multilateral
agencies (such as the IMF and the World Bank) and some 1,400
private banks. The potential risks to the world financial system of
such defaults are, according to Paul Volcker, chairman of the Federal
Reserve, the US's central bank, 'without precedent in the post-war
world.'

Although it was Mexico's inability to service its foreign loans that
made the debt crisis front page news throughout the world, warning
bells had been ringing for some time. The rapid expansion of foreign
debt owed by the less-developed countries (LDCs) since the mid-1970s
had been dramatic. In the mid-1960s LDCs' long (more than five
years) and medium-term debt (one to five years) stood at US$50
billion. By 1976, it had risen to US$200 billion and, by 1981, it totalled
US$500 billion. It is estimated that, in January 1983, LDCs' foreign

*US$1 billion = US$1,000 million.

1

debt, including short-term debt (debt due to mature within one year) and trade credit, was no less than US$700 billion. This is the equivalent of US$150 for every person on earth!

Further analysis of the debt figures gives an indication of the dimensions of the present crisis. For instance, it should be born in mind that the amount of funds available in the hands of private banks for all their foreign lending is US$1,000 billion. Therefore, 70 per cent of this total is consumed by LDC debt. The value of the entire annual production of British industry and commerce (equivalent to a figure of US$500 billion) would not be enough to pay off all LDC debt. For the individual countries concerned, debt servicing (the costs of principal and annual interest payments) represents a crippling burden. Brazil, for example, will have to pay about US$31 billion to service its debt in 1983. This figure represents 117 per cent of the estimated value of all Brazilian exports for the year. As it is from exports that a country earns the foreign exchange needed to meet its overseas obligations (paying for imports and repaying loans), it is clear that Brazil will need to borrow more, just to meet its debt service obligations, before it even considers how to pay for the imports needed to sustain its economy. Brazil is not an isolated example. Mexico will pay 126 per cent of its estimated export revenue on debt servicing in 1983, Argentina 153 per cent, Venezuela 101 per cent and Bolivia 118 per cent.

Although statistics from the 1930s are not directly comparable with present-day figures, it is worth noting that, even in the worst years of the great depression in the 1930s, Brazil's debt servicing as a percentage of its export earnings did not exceed 45 per cent. The corresponding figure for Argentina did not exceed 30 per cent.

Finally, if total foreign debt is expressed in terms of debt per head of population, this would be equivalent to every Brazilian owing over US$700, every Mexican owing over US$1,000 and every Argentinian owing nearly US$1,500!

Background to the Crisis

Although the causes of the current debt crisis are to be found in the deep recession that is affecting the Western world, its roots are firmly embedded in a world economic order that has led to chronic balance of payments deficits for most LDCs, even when the world economy is booming. Their precarious financial position leaves them particularly exposed when recession hits.

The quadrupling of oil prices in 1973 threw a huge burden on the non-oil exporting LDCs, which had to borrow heavily to pay for their

DEBT FIGURES, RESCHEDULING & IMF ASSISTANCE — 1982/3

	Total Debt (US$ billion) 1982 (1)	Short-term Debt (US$ billion) 1982 (2)	Debt Service in 1983 as a % of exports (3)	Sum Rescheduled (US$ billion May 1983) (4)	IMF Assistance (US$ billion May 1983) (5)
Argentina	38.5	19.0	154	5.5[+]	1.6 (standby — 15 months)[+] 0.5 Compensatory Financing Facility
Brazil	84.0	19.0	117	4.7	4.9 Extended Fund Facility[+] 0.5 Compensatory Financing Facility
Mexico	80.0	31.0	126	19.7[+]	3.8 Extended Fund Facility
Total	**202.5[1]**	**69.0[2]**	**—**	**29.9**	**10.3**
Chile	17.0	5.0	104	3.4[+]	0.5 (standby — 2 years)[+] 0.3 Compensatory Financing Facility
Costa Rica	3.5	0.8	n.a.	0.7[+]	0.1 (standby)
Colombia	10.3	4.0	95	—	—
Ecuador	6.5	2.5	102	2.9[+]	0.2 (standby — 1 year)
Peru	11.00	4.8	79	0.3[+]	—
Uruguay	3.5	n.a.	n.a.	0.8[+]	0.4 (standby — 2 years)
Venezuela	28.5	15.0	101	13.0	—
Total (10 countries)	**282.8**	**101.1**	**—**	**51.0**	**11.5**

[+] still being processed.
[1] represents 68% of total for whole of Latin America.
[2] represents 66% of total for whole of Latin America.

Sources: Columns (1) and (2) — Table 3 in Statistical Appendix. (3) — Morgan Guaranty Trust 'World Financial Markets', February 1983. (4) and (5) — Latin America Weekly Report WR-83-19 (20 May, 1983).

oil imports. The impact was most strongly felt by the poor, who faced growing unemployment and reduced social services as governments made the savings needed to meet their oil bills. However, according to the Bank of England, such countries did not face 'unmanageable debt burdens' as a result. Two factors staved off the sort of debt crisis that the world now faces. The first was a short boom in raw material prices on the back of the oil price rise, increasing the value of many LDC exports. The second was the recycling of the surpluses that the oil-producing countries generated back to the countries needing to borrow to pay for their oil, at interest rates that were very low in real terms. This recycling was done by private commercial banks, rather than by any governmental or multilateral agency. The effect of the first oil shock was therefore to increase both non-oil LDC debt and the share of that debt owed to the private banks. From 1965 to 1976, the percentage of Latin American debt owed to commercial banks quadrupled from 12 to 47 per cent.

The second oil price shock of 1979-80, which swelled the oil-producers' balance of payments surpluses by a further US$100 billion, nearly doubled the deficits of the non-oil LDCs from US$45 billion in 1979 to US$88 billion in 1981. This time, the IMF did attempt to increase its lending to help those countries whose balance of payments deficits had become unmanageable. However, the funds it had available were insufficient, given the enormity of the deficits that oil importers faced, and its attempts to obtain more resources were blocked by the new US administration of President Ronald Reagan. The private banks were able, therefore, to step in once again and increase their loans to already heavily endebted LDCs. Non-oil LDC debt rose once again and the proportion of that debt owed to the private banks rose to 55 per cent. After allowing for inflation, the banks had doubled their lending to LDCs in five years.

The implication of this increased reliance on private banks as a source of foreign credits became critical for the LDCs as the economic recession bit more deeply. In contrast to multilateral lenders, 75 per cent of bank credit is at floating rates of interest and therefore becomes more expensive as interest rates rise. The world recession has been accompanied by an interest rate explosion. The rate of interest that LDCs have to pay for their bank loans is determined by the London Interbank Offer Rate (LIBOR), the rate that one bank must pay to borrow funds from another bank. When a bank lends to an LDC customer, it lends money that it has borrowed from a range of other banks. Therefore, LIBOR is the base against which the interest rate the LDC must pay is calculated. LIBOR has risen from 6 per cent in the mid-1970s to an average of 16.5 per cent in 1981, peaking at no less than 19 per cent. It is estimated that each one per cent rise in interest rates adds over US$6 billion to LDC debt bills.

Although nominal interest rates fell in early 1983, real interest rates, that is rates adjusted for inflation, remain high. In the mid-1970s, high inflation and low interest rates meant that real interest rates were usually negative. LDCs were effectively paid to borrow, and they responded by contracting large debts. However, by early 1983, although rates had dropped considerably, inflation had also dropped and the net effect was to leave real interest rates at the historically high figure of 8 per cent.

Not only do LDCs have to pay more for their foreign loans, but the world recession has reduced the prices that they can obtain for their commodity exports. They therefore have to borrow more to cover their shortfalls in export income. It is estimated that, between 1980 and 1982, world commodity prices dropped by 35 per cent to their lowest levels for 30 years. Mr Tom Clausen, the President of the World Bank, has stated that, since 1980, no less than 90 per cent of the long and medium-term bank loans that the LDCs have contracted were needed to cover the fall in their annual export earnings.

By themselves, these falls in commodity prices would not matter if the prices of the goods LDCs need to import were also falling by corresponding amounts. This, however, is not the case. The price of non-oil LDC imports continue to rise, even though the prices of their exports are falling. For example, in 1960, one ton of coffee would buy over 37 tons of fertiliser. Today, the same ton of coffee will buy only 15.8 tons of fertiliser. In 1959, a small truck could be bought with the proceeds of the sale of six tons of jute fibre. Today, a small truck would require the sale of 26 tons of jute. And, whereas in 1960, 6.3 tons of oil could be bought for one ton of sugar, by 1982, the same sugar could buy only 0.7 tons of oil.

The LDCs' problems do not end with the fall in the value of their commodity exports. According to the General Agreement on Tariffs and Trade (GATT, a multilateral agency set up to encourage countries to remove barriers to free trade), increased protectionism by the developed countries is leading to both falling prices for LDC exports and growth in barter trade. Up to 30 per cent of world trade is now done by barter or 'countertrade'. This means that a country selling goods must agree to be 'paid' in other goods, rather than in money. This reduces the LDCs' ability to build up a trading surplus of foreign currency from which to meet their debt payments.

As it became increasingly obvious that the recession was creating a critical situation for many LDCs, the banks began to fear that they would be unable to collect their debts. Their first reaction was to shorten the term of any new lending. Short-term loans are seen as less risky by the banks because their repayment does not rely upon the long-term solvency of the LDCs (which is currently in doubt) and because they allow the banks to collect in their loans rapidly if they themselves face heavy withdrawals by their depositors. Thus LDCs were forced to incur short-term debt in order to pay off longer-term loans and to meet current deficits. This shortening of debt maturity periods was such that, in 1982, long-term debt repayments amounted to US$44 billion while short-term debts maturing during the year amounted to US$140 billion. As short-term debt must be constantly renegotiated or rolled over (that is replacing a maturing short-term loan with a new loan), its withdrawal causes almost immediate cash-flow problems for borrowers. And, as the bank began to lose confidence in the ability of certain LDCs to repay their existing loans, short-term credit began to dry up. Thus, while new bank lending to non-oil LDCs rose by US$150 billion in 1981, and by US$13 billion in the second quarter of 1982, it actually fell in the final quarter of 1982 by US$800 million. This was the first absolute fall since 1977.

Mexico was caught spectacularly in this credit trap. Confidence in its ability to repay its foreign debts was severely shaken when the fall in oil prices began to hit its foreign exchange earnings and inflation began to rise to alarming levels. *The Economist* predicted that Mexico would lose US$2.5 billion in export earnings if oil prices were to drop by US$5 per barrel. The credit needed to roll over its US$40 billion of short-term debts maturing in 1982 was not made available and the country was forced to declare that it could not meet its commitments. There was a near-panic among international lenders. In the scramble to avoid being caught by other defaulting countries, the small banks in particular withdrew their funds from the international loan market. It was precisely this action that brought Brazil, Argentina and a host of other countries to the brink of bankruptcy.

The Fear of Default

The risks for a heavily-indebted LDC in defaulting on its foreign debt obligations are enormous. The refusal to repay or renegotiate any loan to a Western bank or multilateral agency would blacklist the country concerned from receiving any new loans from the entire Western financial establishment. Very soon, the country would run out of the foreign currency needed to pay for its imports and effectively it would have to stop trading. Any assets it held abroad would be seized (as in the case of Iran in 1979) against its unpaid debts. As imports dried up, the country would find itself short of the inputs needed to sustain its industry and agriculture and, in many cases, without sufficient food for its population. Such shortages would have profound social and political consequences within the country.

However, it is not the problems that defaulting countries would face that has generated near-panic in the Western financial community. Rather, it is the fear that a large default would deliver, in the words of *The Economist*, 'a horrendous jolt to the world's banking system'. To understand how Brazil or Mexico could acquire the power to deal such a 'horrendous jolt', we need to look more closely at the nature of the world financial system.

The backbone of the system is the private commercial banks. They aim to maximise their profits by taking deposits and lending them at higher rates of interest. Their security is based on their equity reserves, that is, their shareholders' risk capital, which is available to repay the banks' depositors even if loans to customers should fail to be repaid. However, in the last 20 years, banks have reduced their ratio of reserves to loans from 9 to 2.6 per cent and it is estimated that, for every US dollar of equity, banks now have US$17.50 of outstanding loans, a figure that rises to US$28 for larger banks. As long as those who lend to, or deposit money with, the bank are confident that outstanding bank loans will be repaid, the bank is safe. However, if it appears that large loans will not be repaid or will be late in being repaid (if a major LDC debtor should default, for example), then those who have deposited money with the bank will lose their confidence in being repaid and will try to withdraw their deposits or will call in their loans. This could in the most extreme situation result in a 'run on the bank', which would drain all its reserves. The bank would then have to cease trading, unable to meet its commitments to depositors and lenders.

This situation is exacerbated by the 'interbank market', effectively the wholesale market for money. This allows banks to borrow from other banks and thus transmit money rapidly from areas of excess saving to borrowers in other countries. Nearly 70 per cent of the loans made in the international money market are in fact made to other banks, which in turn lend the money to their own LDC customers. This interlocking system can transmit problems rapidly throughout the whole market. If any particular bank were to lose the confidence of other banks in the interbank market (due to problems with its LDC debt), that bank would find it harder to continue borrowing from other banks to meet its commitments. As many interbank loans are for very short periods, they need to be routinely renewed at maturity. This usually automatic renewal process would stop and the bank concerned would be unable to meet its obligations to its depositors and to other banks from which it had borrowed. These latter banks would then have to scramble to borrow funds from other sources to meet their own commitments and would cut off further lending to other banks until their own position were stabilised. This process would continue on down the chain and could well affect the vast majority of banks in the interbank market, even though they might not actually have loans outstanding to the defaulting country. Thus, panic is caused by the rapid contraction of funds available for lending in the market. It is estimated that a previous bank collapse, that of the Herstatt Bank in 1974, caused a short-term contraction in the international loan market of 50 per cent. It was precisely the contraction in the market following the Mexican crisis that caused the Brazilian liquidity crisis.

The stresses within the banking community have become more apparent in the wake of the Mexican crisis. The smaller or so-called 'regional' banks, those whose activities are confined to one country or region and whose total loans are worth less than US$5 billion, have been sucked into large LDC loans by contributing to the international loans organised or 'syndicated' by the large banks. The prestige of the larger members of the syndicate gave confidence to the smaller regional members. However, debt rescheduling (the process of renegotiating interest rates and repayment terms on outstanding debt) by the large debtor nations has so frightened the regional banks that many now wish to pull out of the international loan market and concentrate on safer, if less profitable, lending business. This would greatly reduce the funds available for international lending.

However, both Mexico and Brazil have required large new bank loans as well as renegotiation of old loans, to tide them over their current problems. This means that unwilling regional banks have been forced to make more international loans in order to save their first loans and protect the financial system. One banker's comment, reported by the *Financial Times,* was: 'We were pretty well told by the Deputy Governor (of the Bank of England) that, if we did not step into line (by agreeing to extra credits for Mexico), . . . our standing in the market would be prejudiced. For the first time in our history as independent bankers, we have been robbed of our freedom of action in taking decisions on whether to make a loan or not.'

And, although the concern of the regional banks is for their own survival, policy-makers are equally concerned with the potentially devastating effects bank closure can have on their own national economies. Not only would bank closures mean substantial losses for those holding bank shares or deposits, but they would also cause serious loss of confidence in other banks that were not necessarily directly affected. These banks could also suffer 'runs on the bank' and possible closure, if the situation were to become serious enough. Even if they were to survive, they would have to call in loans and cut down their new lending to ensure enough liquidity to meet the demands of

Brazil at the Brink

The Brazilian effort to renegotiate its foreign debt of over US$80 billion in the wake of the Mexican debt crisis at the end of 1982, has failed both financially and politically. In a country where 47 per cent of families live below the poverty line and 67 per cent of workers earn less than the equivalent of US$80 a month, there is little surplus to be squeezed out to pay foreign creditors. The riots in April 1983 in São Paulo illustrate the effects of austerity measures on those who have nothing left to lose.

The first IMF agreement for a massive US$6.6 billion loan was negotiated at the end of 1982 and accompanied by a rescheduling of the country's loans from foreign banks in early 1983. Brazil needed an extra US$4.4 billion in new bank loans to see it over its severe liquidity crisis. The success of the package hinged both on Brazil earning a US$6 billion export surplus in 1983 and on the willingness of the banks (especially the smaller regional banks) to continue lending and even to expand their loans. Neither of these conditions was achieved. Despite severe spending cuts, which exacerbated unemployment and reduced government social services, by May 1983 the financial rescue package was in tatters.

There was a violent reaction to the austerity programme imposed by the IMF, manifested on the streets of São Paulo in April 1983. But the IMF decided on 18 May to stop all further drawings by Brazil because government spending was still beyond the IMF targets. In order to regain the confidence of funders, the government rapidly drew up an emergency package of drastic cuts in investment in public companies (thus increasing unemployment), increases in the prices of petrol and wheat, changes in wage policy for state employees and cuts in agricultural subsidies.

By early July, it appeared that the government felt it had done enough to meet the IMF's conditions and was taking a hard line against further cuts. It warned the Fund of the political repercussions that would follow any further cuts in government expenditure. As negotiations dragged on, a large strike by the Oil Workers' Union of Campinas, was broken up by the army and the strike leaders were imprisoned. Support for the strikers was headed off by the right-wing leadership of the country's other unions because the latter feared a complete military take-over if the unions took to the streets.

Ironically, the hard line military action against the strikers lost the government a negotiating card *vis-à-vis* the IMF. The threat of large-scale social unrest having been repressed, at least momentarily, the IMF pressed the Bank for International Settlements to refuse to roll over its US$400 million bridging loan in order to force the country to

⬦

accept further IMF austerity measures. Despite the talk of a moratorium on foreign debt repayments, the Brazilian government acceded to the Fund's demands. In an effort to reduce inflation and government spending, the government ordered wage cuts of 30 per cent breaking the link whereby wages had to keep pace with the rise in the price index. *Time* magazine suggested: 'Brazil's military leaders may decide to exercise more direct control over the government and bring the country's tiptoeing toward democracy, or *abertura,* to a screeching halt'. The conditions now being demanded by the IMF are so onerous that the Governor of Brazil's central bank, Carlos Langoni, has resigned in protest. He described the conditions as 'un-realisable!'

their depositors. This would mean falling profits. For the country as a whole, falling bank credit would lead to falling demand and, at worst, to bankruptcies and lay-offs.

Thus the problems in Mexico City and Brasília can have a direct bearing on the economic welfare of the British High Street. So why have the banks exposed themselves to these dangers? According to US Senator John Heinz, the banks have only themselves to blame. 'I believe', he told a congressional hearing at the end of 1982, 'that the banks have been imprudent and more than just a little greedy.' Lending in the international money market offers high returns that most banks have been unable to resist. Large 'spreads' (that is the difference between LIBOR and the rate of interest paid by the borrower) and instant fees (up to US$1.25 million on every US$1 billion lent) have resulted in very high bank profits. Citicorp, one of the largest US banking companies, increased its profits from its Brazilian lendings by 46 per cent in one year and that one country now generates 20 per cent of Citicorp's world-wide profits. Brazil is five times more profitable than any of the company's other lending operations. Mexico, the *Financial Times* reported, faces fees of almost US$200 million for its rescheduling operation and will end up paying so much more for its new bank credit that, 'for many banks, it will almost double the return on assets earned from Mexico'.

Citicorp is by no means an isolated example. Lloyds Bank International, in announcing quadrupled profits in the half-year beginning in September 1982, noted that a major boost to its profits came from countries such as Mexico which were rescheduling their debts. The bank's lending to Latin America, some £3.5 billion, earned interest charges of £138 million, up from £29 million in the previous half year. Finally, Libra Bank, the largest London bank specialising in lending to Latin America, reported profits up by 30 per cent in its latest annual report and it now ranks as one of the most profitable banks in the world.

OUTSTANDING BANK LOANS TO LATIN AMERICA

US BANKS (US$ billion)

	Brazil	Mexico	Venezuela	Others+	Total	Total as % of Banks' Equity
Citicorp	4.4	3.3	1.1	1.1	9.8	203
Bank America	2.3	2.5	2.0	0	6.8	148
Chase Manhattan	2.4	1.7	1.0	1.0	6.1	222
Man. Hanover	2.0	1.7	1.1	2.0	6.8	245
Morgan Guaranty	1.7	1.1	0.5	0.8	4.1	150

+ Includes disclosed exposure of more than 1% to Argentina, Yugoslavia and Chile.

Source: The American Banker (quoted in *The New York Times,* 18 March 1983).

BRITISH BANKS (£ billion)

	Total Loans to Latin America	Equity Reserves	Total as % of Banks' Equity
Barclays	2.3	2.9	79
Nat. Westminster	1.8	2.6	69
Midland	3.6	2.0	180
Lloyds	3.6	2.0	180

Source: Published Accounts and International Bank Credit Analysis (quoted in the *Financial Times,* 31 May 1983).

According to a report presented to the Conference of Non-Aligned Nations in Havana in 1983, the 'export of capital has become the most lucrative form of capital investment in the Third World'. Here lies the key to understanding the debt crisis. The banks have been pushing to expand their lending to LDC customers in order to take advantage of the very high profits involved. They have now pushed so hard that, in the context of the current world recession, they have left themselves without adequate reserves to pay their depositors should outstanding loans fail to be repaid, and they have left many LDCs unable to meet their loan servicing obligations. Far from fulfilling the normal image

11

of risk-avoiding, conservative bankers, they have taken huge risks in order to increase their profits massively.

It is against this background of imprudent lending and the potential threat it poses to lenders that the present fear of default must be analysed. Recognising the leverage that being a huge debtor affords, Brazil, for example, drew up its own rescheduling programme before consulting its lenders. As *The Sunday Times* observed, 'Brazil's decision to take unilateral action marks the first attempt by a major debtor nation to impose its own terms on creditors rather than wait for a formal debt rescheduling. Bankers fear it could set a dangerous precedent for other nations with large debts'.

It is to resolve this contradiction between what is traditionally viewed as the acceptable, individually profit maximising Western banks and the unacceptable, the threat to international financial stability that their collective action represents, that the role of the International Monetary Fund enters the picture.

The Debt Crisis and the IMF

The IMF is seen as pivotal to the world economic system and crucial to the West's efforts to resolve the current debt crisis. The original purposes of the IMF are summed up in Article One of the Articles of Agreement under which the IMF was established on 27 December 1945. Its overall aim is to facilitate the growth of world trade, which it is argued is fundamental to the need to generate 'high levels of employment and real income and the development of the productive resources of all members . . .' One of the main ways that this is achieved is through IMF loans to those countries that are unable to earn enough foreign currency to pay for the imports they need.

The essence of the debt crisis for the West is that heavily indebted LDCs cannot earn enough foreign currency from their exports to meet their debt obligations and it is the inability of LDCs to earn such foreign currency to pay for their imports and debt repayments that has put a strain on the world banking system. It is essential, if the present system is to continue, that such LDCs be able to borrow more funds to return themselves to solvency in the short term and thus to maintain the solvency of their creditors. But they must also make appropriate changes to their internal economies so that they will generate enough foreign exchange to meet their debt service obligations in the long run. The banks are unable to fulfill these two conditions. Rather than increase their lending to deficit LDCs, many are trying to reduce that lending and individually reduce the risk they face in being over-exposed to potentially defaulting debtors.

The IMF has the authority to impose conditions on deficit LDCs and, in a crisis, on the private banks as well. Firstly, it is a multilateral agency, made up of representatives of 147 nations and charged with ensuring financial stability. When it speaks, it claims to do so on behalf of governments and therefore has the authority to impose conditions on governments that are themselves represented within the IMF. Secondly, it is the 'lender of last resort' for deficit countries. This gives it the same sort of power as, for example, a pawnbroker might exercise over an individual who could no longer obtain credit from his or her bank or local shop. Just as the pawnbroker imposes severe conditions, the deposit of valuables in exchange for the loan and severe default penalties (the forfeit of the valuables), so the IMF can demand wide-ranging conditions in terms of changes in economic policy (reduced government spending, devaluation, reducing imports) in exchange for its credit. As the credit provided by the IMF is as important to the banks (it ensures that their loans will continue to be repaid) as it is to the LDC, the banks are also prepared to accept some degree of IMF authority in terms of extending their loans and lending new money.

Thirdly, IMF power goes beyond its ability to lend. Because it is seen as the regulatory back-stop of the financial system, the ultimate financial authority to be exercised in times of crisis, the rest of the financial community will not lend to a deficit country unless it has received the IMF 'seal of approval'. That seal of approval is only given to countries prepared to accept the changes in their economic policy that the IMF demands. The IMF is, therefore, the key that can open the door to the international loans that most LDCs need to keep afloat.

This crucial role of police-officer of the international financial system underlines the power that the IMF exercises. Although it is that debt crisis that has made the IMF front-page news around the world, its importance goes beyond the resolution of that crisis. As most LDCs face chronic balance of payments deficits due to the model of development that they adopt, they have to call repeatedly on the rich Western nations for financial support. The IMF is the channel that Western nations use to supply that financial support and impose the conditions on deficit countries that reinforce those development strategies approved by the West. Thus the IMF is one of the key instruments in determining how LDCs approach their development problems.

Chapter Two of *The Poverty Brokers* will look more closely at how the IMF works and at the development strategies it promotes. It will explain how the IMF is controlled, who exercises that control and who benefits from the policies it adopts.

In Chapter Three, the IMF view of the world will be examined from the point of view of the needs of the poor majority who live in the LDCs, and who are usually the most adversely affected by IMF policies.

This will be followed by three case studies which examine the effects IMF programmes have had in Chile, Jamaica and Peru. It is only by assessing the long-term impact of IMF policies that their full effects on LDC development can be understood. The case studies paint a picture of long-term decline in employment, falling production and increased impoverishment for the majority of the people.

The final chapter looks at different proposals suggested for both the resolution of the debt crisis and for reform of the IMF. It argues that, as the IMF is an important instrument used by the powerful Western nations to maintain the existing financial order, it cannot be instrumental in fundamentally changing that order. The IMF will only take on a new role as a consequence of fundamental changes in power relations between nations and between different groups of people within nations.

2 The IMF's view of the World

'The IMF's arrival on the scene has brought a healthy dose of sound financial sense to economies whose direction has for long been dictated by local policies. The IMF's three main macroeconomic prescriptions for the Latin American countries have been admirable. They are:
1. A reduction in government budget deficits.
2. Limits to money supply growth in order to bring inflation down.
3. A policy of currency depreciation to achieve balance of payments improvements without contributing too much to inflation.'

The Economist, April 1983.

The organisation of an international monetary system is a complex problem. Historically, all international transactions had ultimately to be conducted in gold since the intrinsic value of the metal could not be counterfeited or reproduced by a government through control over the printing press. The use of gold was also a guarantee to the selling country that it was receiving a means of payment which it would subsequently be able to use to buy goods from any other country in the world. But gold is an expensive and cumbersome form of money. It is expensive to produce, and is difficult and risky to transport around the world to settle international debts. Nor can its supply be easily adjusted when growing world trade requires an increase in world liquidity. Thus it was desirable that countries should find some way of using paper or token money to settle their external debts, as is customary with internal transactions. This, however, raised a serious problem. People could rely on paper money for internal transactions because the state intervened to guarantee the value of the currency and to force everyone to accept it. But internationally people were trading between countries with different currencies whose value in relation to each other could be altered at will by the respective governments. In the 1930s, indeed, countries did devalue their currencies to gain competitive advantages over each other without consultation. As a result, trade became increasingly difficult and both individuals and countries became unwilling to hold foreign currencies for any longer than was absolutely necessary.

Thus, in order to create a reliable system, there had to be some means to ensure that countries would allow their currencies to be exchanged on a stable basis with the currencies of those countries with which they were trading. While this would facilitate bilateral trade, in order for multilateral trade to occur it was also necessary to ensure that all countries would be willing to allow their currencies to be freely converted into all other currencies. Where such convertibility exists, it becomes possible for any country to pay for its imports with currencies earned from its exports to any other country in the system. In this way, it will not have to export directly to any country in order to be able to import from it, making much more flexible trading relationships possible.

This system of multilateral trade depends on all countries keeping their balance of payments in equilibrium, so as to obviate the necessity for access to foreign loans to pay for those imports not covered by export earnings. Any country which continues to run a deficit for very long would exhaust its supplies of foreign currency and be unable to pay for its imports. The value of its currency would decline in relation to those of the countries from which it was importing, and it would be tempted to impose protective tariffs on further imports. Thus to maintain the stability of the international monetary system, and to stop countries from adopting trade protection policies because of short-term balance of payments problems, it was necessary to create some means of supplying foreign reserves to those countries running balance of payments deficits.

The Bretton Woods Solution

After the Second World War, a number of leading politicians and administrators felt that some form of international organisation should be set up to avoid a reversion to the protectionism of the 1930s and to enable the international monetary system to be organised on an agreed basis. Such an organisation would first of all ensure that a stable currency which could be used by all countries for their international transactions was available. That currency would also provide sufficient world liquidity to facilitate the non-inflationary expansion of world trade. Secondly, it would ensure that all countries abided by an agreed set of rules to regulate their monetary relations with other countries. Thirdly, it would make available some form of financial assistance to countries with balance of payments difficulties so that they would not have to resort to protectionism.

The purpose of the IMF

The articles of agreement which brought the International Monetary Fund into being were agreed on 27 December 1945 at a meeting attended by representatives of the allied governments in Washington. Article 1 which laid out the purpose of the Fund is quoted here in full.

'The International Monetary Fund is established and shall operate in accordance with the following provisions:

Article 1 Purposes

The purposes of the International Monetary Fund are:

i. To promote international monetary co-operation through a permanent institution which provides for consultation and collaboration on international problems.
ii. To facilitate the expansion and balanced growth of international trade and to contribute thereby to the promotion and maintenance of high levels of employment and real income and the development of the productive resources of all members as primary objectives of economic policy.
iii. To promote exchange stability, to maintain orderly exchange arrangements among members and to avoid competitive exchange depreciation.
iv. To assist in the establishment of a multilateral system of payments in respect of current transactions between members and in the elimination of foreign exchange restrictions which hamper the growth of world trade.
v. To give confidence to members by making the Fund's resources available to them under adequate safeguards, thus providing them with the opportunity to correct maladjustments in their balance of payments without resorting to measures destructive of national or international prosperity.
vi. In accordance with the above to shorten the duration and lessen the degree of disequilibrium in the international balances of payments of members.'

The full text of the Articles of Agreement was published by HMSO, Treaty Series No 21 (Cmnd 6885) 1946.

The IMF: Time for Reform, N. Butler.

Various proposals were made during the latter part of the Second World War, the most far-reaching of which came from J.M. Keynes, probably the most influential economist of the period. These proposals were then debated at a conference which took place at Bretton Woods in the United States in 1944. The IMF and World

Bank were formally established a year later. The IMF's primary responsibility was to deal with monetary matters and particularly with countries suffering from short-term balance of payments problems. The World Bank was established to provide long-term developmental assistance to both developed and developing countries.

The IMF was brought into existence on the basis of a set of Articles of Agreement which laid down the conditions all countries had to accept in international monetary relationships. The most important of these related to the problems of exchange rates and convertibility mentioned above. The original agreements required all countries to endeavour to maintain stable exchange rates. Changes could only be made after prior consultation with the IMF. Secondly, they required all countries to establish fully convertible currencies to maximise the possibility for unfettered multilateral trade. Further, as a condition of membership, all countries were required to contribute a quota to the Fund of which about 25 per cent had to be in gold, and the rest in its own currency. These resources provide the basis for the 'stand-by' programmes which the IMF negotiates with countries in balance of payment difficulties.

Thus, to understand the role of the IMF, we have to understand the way in which it deals with:
    a. exchange rate control.
    b. the convertibility of currencies.
    c. the provision of balance of payments financing.
    d. control over the supply of world liquidity.

Exchange rate control

At the end of the war the US dominated the world economy. It controlled 70 per cent of the world's gold reserves and a major part of its functioning industrial capacity. It had by then displaced Britain as the central country in the financial system. The dollar had become the main currency in which international transactions were made and thus the main source of international liquidity. The value of the dollar was directly related to gold (at US$35 per oz). The gold price was fixed after the US agreed to buy the whole supply at that price, and dollars could be exchanged for gold by foreign bankers who preferred to hold gold rather than dollars. Thus everyone believed that they could rely on the dollar as a stable currency, partly because they knew that they could use their dollars to obtain gold and partly because they trusted the US government to ensure that gold would not depreciate in value. The value of all other currencies were consequently determined by their rate of exchange against the dollar — a rate that governments were expected to maintain except in cases of 'fundamental disequilibrium'. To maintain such stability they would have to keep their exports and imports in balance, either by maintaining an adequate level of exports, or by borrowing a sufficient amount to cover any excess of imports. If they failed to maintain this balance the value of their currency would decline and they would be forced to spend their foreign reserves in supporting its value. Once this process reached a certain point, the currency would probably have to be devalued in order to increase exports so as to earn more foreign currency to pay for imports.

This system of relatively fixed exchange rates (the 'adjustable peg' system) survived more or less intact until the early 1970s. Immediately after the war, most countries were part of various colonial empires and did not have their own national currencies. Third World countries which did have such currencies — for example, the Latin American countries — usually tied their value to one or other of the currencies of the leading countries. The industrialised countries initially found that their currencies were over-valued in relation to the dollar, and a general devaluation took place in 1949. Thereafter, stability was sustained until the late 1960s. In the Third World, on the other hand, a number of devaluations took place during the 1950s (for example, in Bolivia, Mexico, Chile and Nicaragua) some of them involving very large changes. These had to be authorised by the IMF, but were all accepted.

Given that none of these countries played a significant part in world trade, these changes could be accepted without affecting the system as a whole. But, in the late 1960s the stability of some of the strong industrial countries became doubtful. In 1967, Britain finally devalued the pound, realising that it could not control its balance of payments deficit by further reducing public spending. In France, the crisis of May 1968 led to large wage increases and forced a devaluation of the franc. However, even these turned out to be minor aberrations when compared to the fundamental problems the dollar was facing. The United States had been running an overall balance of payments deficit since 1947, due largely to military spending abroad and foreign investment by US corporations. This deficit had initially been covered by the country's large reserves. But these had been greatly reduced by the end of the 1960s, and the escalation of the war in Vietnam led only to a further worsening of the deficit. In 1971, President Nixon announced both that the US would no longer be willing to convert the dollar into gold and that the dollar would be devalued. The subsequent devaluation was not large enough and the deficit continued, leading to a further and larger devaluation against other leading currencies in 1973.

Thus, in one single announcement, the US toppled two fundamental pillars of the Bretton Woods agreement, fixed exchange parities and gold as the common denominator of the system. It became impossible to maintain stable exchange rates in the face of the dollar devaluation and currencies began to move rapidly one against another. The system was out of control.

The response of the major industrialised countries, which met as the so-called Group of Ten was to recognise that 'floating rates' had become a reality and suggested merely that central banks should endeavour to manage the floating so as to avoid rapid changes. As the value of the dollar was no longer fixed to gold, its value was now measured in terms of other currencies.

Convertibility of currencies

The second important area of concern for the IMF relates to the convertibility of currencies. Immediately after the war all countries (except the US and Switzerland) imposed severe limits on the convertibility of their currencies, making it possible for them to restrict access to foreign exchange and thereby to impose close controls over trade and the balance of payments. These limits applied to the currency required for both capital and current account transactions that were needed to make overseas investments or to pay for imported goods. Without these controls, the central bank of any country could exert no direct control over the balance of payments; with them, it could limit the supply of foreign exchange to importers and thus intervene directly to limit trade when a balance of payments deficit seemed imminent.

Given the basic commitment of the IMF to liberalise trade, the founders of the organisation, and the US in particular, wanted to see these controls eliminated as soon as possible. On the other hand, it was accepted that none of the countries whose economies had been destroyed by the war could afford to allow free convertibility until they had rebuilt their industries to the point where they could compete successfully.

Thus the IMF allowed countries in this position to retain currency restrictions during a 'transitional period' until they were able to compete, but expected that they should then 'take all possible measures' to abolish them. Countries still imposing these controls fell under Article XIV of the IMF constitution. Those which had done away with them agreed to accept Article VIII, which ruled out the right to 'impose restrictions on the making of payments and transfers for current international transactions'. Once a country had moved from Article XIV to Article VIII status, there was no right to revert. This regulation did not exclude the use of controls to limit transfers for capital investment; Britain, for example, ended convertibility at the end of the 1950s but only lifted capital controls in 1979. However, most of the leading industrial countries adopted full convertibility at the end of the 1950s, once they felt they were strong enough to compete successfully with the US.

Financing balance of payments deficits

Thirdly, the IMF has the power to lend money to countries which need to overcome short-term balance of payments problems. The main form in which such credit is provided is through so-called stand-by agreements, where the size of the potential contribution is determined by the size of the country's 'quota' contribution to the Fund. Since it is the negotiations surrounding these agreements that have been the subject of much of the political controversy over the work of the fund during the past decade, it is worth considering this issue in some detail.

At Bretton Woods, Keynes, leading the British delegation, argued that the new international organisation should have the power to borrow money on a large scale from the reserves of the countries which had balance of payments surpluses and to lend it for developmental projects to countries which were in deficit. In this way, he felt, the possibility of international recessions could be avoided and weak countries would always be able to avoid having to adopt deflationary or protectionist policies. The US (whose surpluses would have been used to provide most of the credit in the first instance) refused to accept the full programme outlined by Keynes and instead accepted a system in which each country would contribute a quota, partly in gold, partly in its own currency. This could then be used for short-term lending (not for anything which approximated to 'development') to help countries adopt policies which would overcome their balance of payments deficits without major disturbances to their international trade.

To ensure that these countries did adopt policies which were internationally acceptable (especially to the surplus countries whose funds were being used to provide them with assistance) the Fund was allowed to impose conditions with respect to the economic policies which the country would have to adopt before it became eligible for the credit. Thus, any country which comes to the Fund for such help (after, that is, it has drawn on the first 25 per cent of its quota, which it can use unconditionally) is expected to receive an IMF delegation which negotiates a 'package' of policies with the government prior to the loan being given. Once the loan has been provided, the country has to allow its policies to be inspected every six months and the support can be withdrawn if the conditions are not being fulfilled. It is this 'conditionality' that gives the Fund its power to influence the internal economic policies of particular countries.

21

Although the amounts of money provided by the IMF stand-by loans are not very large, the exercise of its supervisory role over LDC economies is undoubtedly important. Most countries rely on the private banks for the bulk of their credit and the banks prefer to lend to countries which have established an effective relationship with the IMF. This serves as a guarantee that countries will adopt policies consistent with repaying their bank loans. The banks themselves find it very difficult to impose economic policies directly on governments, a lesson that was brought home to them in the mid-1970s when they attempted to force the government of Peru to adopt an austerity programme which was so severe as to be unacceptable. They were then forced to bring in the IMF, which eventually established an agreed programme upon which the banks were willing to continue lending.

Thus, there is a real sense in which the IMF performs the role of disciplining countries which fail to keep control over their balance of payments, a role which was formerly performed by one or other of the colonial powers. 'Gunboat diplomacy' has now given way to 'IMF diplomacy', with the threat of an end to the vital borrowing which comes from both the Fund and the private banks once an agreement has been successfully reached. The failure to secure foreign credits usually means a period of severely restricted consumption for the country concerned and real difficulty in obtaining essential equipment and spares for industry, trade and the social services.

Control over the supply of world liquidity
One important aim outlined for the IMF at Bretton Woods was that it should seek to regulate the supply of internationally usable money to the world economy so as to avoid a constriction in world growth (if too little world liquidity were available) and international inflation (if too much liquidity were available). This meant either controlling the US balance of payments deficit, which flooded dollars onto the world market, or introducing a world currency that could be used for international transactions and whose supply could be controlled by a multilateral central bank.

However, these ideas were vigorously opposed by the US, which benefited from its ability to run large balance of payments deficits without the risk of having to devalue its currency. This was because other nations of the world were willing to hold dollars as, so they hoped, a stable reserve currency based on the strength of the US economy. Therefore, an ever-growing US balance of payments deficit, caused by large overseas military expenditure, foreign investment and a worsening trade balance, resulted in large quantities of dollars being pumped into the world system and thus contributed to the high levels of inflation that existed during the 1960s and 1970s. When the US acted to reduce its deficit, world liquidity was reduced dramatically, and growth rates tumbled.

The IMF was powerless to control the US actions because the latter, with far more votes within the governing body of the IMF than any other nation, could veto any attempt to regulate the flow of dollars or to replace the dollar by a multilaterally controlled alternative source of liquidity. Although the IMF did have an alternative source of international money, the Special Drawing Rights (a form of credit issued by the IMF, with which countries could meet their international debts), the quantity of SDRs created (the equivalent of approximately US$9 billion from 1970 to 1972 and US$12 billion from 1978 to 1980) was insufficient to make any impact on overall world liquidity. Thus the IMF has been unable to influence overall world liquidity.

How the IMF Operates

Although it is usual to speak of the IMF 'lending' money to support countries with balance of payments deficits, this is not strictly correct. A deficit country is one that has been unable to earn enough foreign currency to meet all its overseas commitments. When this happens, the IMF sells foreign currency to the debtor nation in exchange for that nation's own currency. This is the process of 'drawing' from the IMF. When the country concerned comes to 'pay back' the IMF, it has to buy back its own currency, paying for it with the hard currencies (or gold) that it has earned abroad.

The funds the IMF has available for members come from three sources. The most important source is the contribution that each member country makes to the fund. Known as the 'quota', this is determined for each country according to its gross national product (GNP, the value of the goods and services that the country produces) and the size of its international trade. The larger the country's economy, the larger its quota contribution. Twenty-five per cent of the quota has to be paid in either Special Drawing Rights or in hard currencies, the latter being the currencies of the economically strong nations which are in demand, either to purchase that country's exports or to act as a reserve of value which, it is hoped, will not be hit by devaluation. The rest can be paid in the country's own currency. The number of votes that each country has in the making of IMF decisions is determined by its quota contribution. Each country has 250 basic votes plus one extra vote for (approximately) each US$100,000 worth of quota contribution. Total IMF quotas are soon to be raised to about US$90 billion.

The second source of funds available are those borrowed either from IMF members (over and above their quota contribution) or from non-members. In 1974-75, and again in 1979 and 1983, the IMF borrowed from a range of countries. The earlier borrowings were to establish the General Agreement to Borrow (GAB) which made funds available only to a small group of rich Western nations. Later borrowings, increasing the GAB from US$7.4 billion to US$17 billion, have now been made available to all IMF members. It is becoming an increasingly important source of IMF resources.

The third type of resources available are the Special Drawing Rights (SDRs) that the IMF allocates to members from time to time. Just as a country's central bank creates money within that country (the quantity depending on the level of economic activity within the country and government policy objectives), so the IMF, in 1970-72 and 1979-80, created a form of international money and distributed it to IMF members. SDRs are not money in the sense that the countries can spend them directly. Rather, they are credits in the countries' accounts with the IMF. They can be used to buy from the IMF the hard currencies that a country needs to pay its foreign debts. In IMF terminology, this is the right to draw against IMF funds, hence the name SDRs.

The value of an SDR was originally set at one US dollar. However, in order to make them independent of the fluctuations in the value of the dollar, they are now valued in relation to the average value of a range of world currencies. In mid-1980, the total value of SDRs allocated was in the region of US$22.5 billion.

The IMF makes funds available to its members through a variety of credit facilities and credit 'tranches' (or credit slices). The limit to which a member may draw is worked out according to its quota contribution and, at the moment, it is equal to four-and-a-half times the quota. As the country draws more heavily on IMF funds, the conditions attached to the drawings become more stringent. A country may draw up to 25 per cent of its quota without conditions. This is called the reserve tranche. The first credit tranche (an extra 25 per cent of the value of the quota) is subject to low conditionality, while the upper credit tranches (extra credit slices, each worth 25 per cent of the members' quota) are subject to full conditionality. These are provided in the form of stand-by arrangements; that is, funds to be drawn over a period of time subject to the country passing a performance test set by the IMF before the next instalment of credit is released.

While the provision of short-term lending through stand-by credits is the main form of IMF funding, several other forms of credit have been brought into existence as a result of pressures from potential borrowers. In the 1960s a fund was created to lend to countries which suffered balance of payments losses as a result of short-term declines

USE OF FUND RESOURCES BY FACILITIES 1974-1981
(In Millions of SDRs)

Type of Transaction	1974	1975	1976	1977	1978	1979	1980	1981
Reserve tranche	607	981	1,324	161	136	2,480	222	474
Credit tranche	239	1,604	461	2,370	1,937	485	1,106	2,682
Buffer stock	—	—	5	—	—	48	26	—
Compensatory financing	212	18	828	1,753	322	465	863	784
Extended facility	—	—	8	190	109	242	216	920
Oil facility	—	2,499	3,966	437	—	—	—	—
Total	**1,058**	**5,102**	**6,592**	**4,911**	**2,504**	**3,720**	**2,433**	**4,860**

Source: IMF Annual Report, 1981, Washington, DC, p.82.

in the prices of particular raw materials. The Compensatory Financing Facility was set up in 1963 and loaned an average of US$51.4 million a year from 1963 to 1971. Also in the late 1960s, when raw material prices were low, the IMF agreed to set up a Buffer Stock Facility intended to provide the credit needed to build up stocks of primary products whose prices were subject to wide fluctuations and for which international intervention was seen as the best method of price control. In this case, it has been very difficult to find commodities for which agreed programmes could be created and very little use has been made of this facility as a result.

In the 1970s, further funds were set up. In 1974, the IMF persuaded a number of oil exporters to lend it the money to set up an Oil Facility intended for loans to countries badly hit by the oil price rise of the previous year. This also included a subsidy to the poorest countries to enable them to meet the interest costs involved. But this was a temporary arrangement which only operated from 1975 to 1977. Also in 1974, in response to the demand for an extension of the stand-by credits period, the Extended Fund Facility was introduced. Finally, during the later 1970s, there was pressure for the creation of a Supplementary Financing Facility which would make resources available to countries which had reached the limits of their quotas and would not otherwise be able to borrow further. The first loans under this facility were made in 1979.

Who Makes the Decisions?

The IMF has a membership of 147 nations, made up of rich Western countries, LDCs and a handful of Eastern Bloc countries including Yugoslavia, Romania, Hungary, China, Vietnam and Laos. All agree to be bound by the Articles of Agreement of the IMF and by the decisions of the governing body concerning policy.

Overall authority within the IMF rests with the governing body, an annual meeting of (usually) the finance ministers of all IMF members. These meetings are general consultations on broad policy issues and do not exercise effective decision-making power. Real power rests in the hands of the Executive Board. At present, the Executive Board has 22 members. Six are appointed, the USA, France, the United Kingdom, West Germany, Japan and Saudi Arabia (a major lender to the Fund), 15 members are elected by various country groupings and vote on behalf of all the countries in their respective groups. China is a permanent member in its own right.

Although decisions within the Executive Board are normally reached by consensus, the weight attached to each member's point of

VOTING POWER IN THE IMF (30 April 1982)

	Votes	Percentage of Fund Total
United States	126,325	19.64
United Kingdom	44,125	6.86
West Germany	32,590	5.07
France	29,035	4.51
Japan	25,135	3.91
Saudi Arabia	21,250	3.30
Total	**278,460**	**43.29**
Costa Rica	865	
El Salvador	895	
Guatemala	1,015	
Honduras	760	
Mexico	8,275	
Nicaragua	760	
Spain	8,605	
Venezuela	10,150	
Sub-Total	**31,325**	**4.87**
Brazil	10,225	
Colombia	3,145	
Dominican Republic	1,075	
Ecuador	1,300	
Guyana	625	
Haiti	595	
Panama	925	
Surinam	625	
Trinidad and Tobago	1,480	
Sub-Total	**19,995**	**3.11**
Argentina	8,275	
Bolivia	925	
Chile	3,505	
Paraguay	595	
Peru	2,710	
Uruguay	1,510	
Sub-Total	**17,520**	**2.72**
Total (excluding Spain)	**60,235**	**9.55**

view reflects the votes they command. Four main voting blocks can be identified. The first is the US, which alone controls 20 per cent of the votes. The second is a group of powerful west European nations, which hold about 28 per cent of the votes. The third is an intermediate group, which includes many LDCs but which are represented on the

Board by rich nations. So, for example, in 1979, Spain represented Costa Rica, El Salvador, Guatemala, Honduras, Mexico, Nicaragua and Venezuela on the Board, despite the fact that Venezuela had a bigger quota contribution than Spain. In fact, it is estimated that 21 LDCs, with more than 7 per cent of IMF votes, were represented by northern countries that year. No LDC represents a group which consists of northern countries. The fourth group are the LDCs (including Saudi Arabia) which control about 34 per cent of total votes.

LDCs therefore can exercise only a very limited influence on the decision-making process, because of their lack of voting strength. A totally united group of LDCs (in practice very hard to achieve) representing nearly 75 per cent of the total population of IMF countries can muster no more than 35 per cent of the votes. Also because major changes in IMF policy, such as the allocation of votes require an 85 per cent majority, one country, the US, has an effective veto.

Although the Executive Board holds decision-making power, the managing director and his staff have considerable influence. It is an uncontested tradition that the Fund's managing director is a west European and that his deputy is a US citizen. Furthermore, the Western Hemisphere Department, which includes Latin America and the Caribbean, has a US citizen as its director.

Discussions concerning international financial affairs also take place outside the confines of the IMF, between groups of like-minded countries. In some cases such discussions, although external to the IMF, have considerable influence on the Fund's policy. The main developed countries meet monthly at the Bank for International Settlements (BIS), which regulates the relations between the central banks of the various countries. They also meet at the Paris Club, an informal gathering of creditor nations (usually the developed nations again), which convene to discuss requests from debtor nations to reschedule their loans outstanding to foreign governments. The Group of Ten, representing the 10 most powerful western nations, meets regularly to decide joint policy on financial issues. Many observers argue that this group, together with the Group of Five (the five Western permanent members of the IMF Executive Board — the US, the UK, France, West Germany and Japan) in fact decides on the policy matters that the Executive Board endorses as official IMF policy. As *The Guardian* concluded: 'If the Group of Five can agree on something, then it will go through'.

The LDCs meet in their own Group of 24, a semi-official body of the IMF that represents their interests. The Group arose out of the Group of 77, the most important LDC forum, which is associated with the United Nations Conference on Trade and Development (UNCTAD) and now consists of more than 100 countries. However, not only does the Group of 24 have very little influence in the IMF, some people argue that it has also distanced itself from its constituency, the Group of 77.

At the end of the day, the LDCs, no matter how they are organised, do not have the voting strength to oppose the policies of the powerful western nations.

3 The World's view of the IMF

'Money is power. This simple truth is valid for national and
international relations. Those who wield power control money. An
international monetary system is both a function and an instrument
of prevailing power structures.'
The Arusha Initiative, 1980.

The IMF maintains that its operations are politically neutral and
based on a scientific assessment of the causes of balance of payments
deficits. Furthermore, IMF conditionality, the conditions a country
must fulfil before it receives the IMF 'seal of approval' is said to be
applied objectively to all deficit countries irrespective of political
considerations. Yet, behind these claims of scientific justification and
political neutrality, the IMF subscribes to a particular economic and
political view of the world. This view argues that free trade and the
unhindered operations of market forces are conducive to the welfare
of the international economy. As Article I of the IMF Articles of
Agreement states, one of the main aims of the fund is to 'facilitate the
expansion and balanced growth of international trade' because, as
President Ronald Reagan argues, 'Free trade serves the cause of
economic progress and it serves the cause of world peace'.

Such views on how economic progress is achieved (and how
economic crises are avoided) are not universally accepted. President
Nyerere of Tanzania stated in 1980: 'I doubt whether there are now
people who honestly believe that the IMF is politically or ideologically
neutral. It has an ideology of economic and social development that it
is trying to impose on poor countries'. The Brandt Commission, in its
first report, argued that the conditions imposed by the IMF on deficit
countries had forced unnecessary and unacceptable political burdens

on the poorest, on occasions leading to 'IMF riots' and even the downfall of governments. In addition, the Arusha Initiative, signed in 1980 by a number of LDC representatives, argues that, far from being scientific and generating economic progress, 'the performance tests which the Fund imposes lack scientific basis' and that 'the Fund policies conceived to achieve stabilisation, have in fact contributed to destabilisation and to the limitation of democratic processes'.

In order to assess the IMF's claim to political neutrality and the different criticisms that are levelled against it, it is important to note that the claims and counterclaims emanate from groups of people who have quite different views on why economic crises occur, how they should be resolved and how economic development could be achieved. Each view is logical within its own framework and has a body of evidence to support its claims. Most importantly, the policy prescriptions associated with each view, when implemented, serve the interests of the group that holds that view.

One strand of economic thought stresses that economic prosperity results from the unhindered operations of market forces. According to Milton Friedman, mentor of the Chicago school of economics, the unregulated action of supply and demand 'can co-ordinate the activities of millions of people, each seeking his own interest, in such a way as to make everyone better off'. Free market competition, including unregulated international trade, will ensure the prosperity of those who produce and sell at the lowest price. The profits generated by these efficient producers will trickle down to all levels of society by way of increased investment (thus creating more employment), higher wages and the payment of more taxes to be used for the provision of essential social services. This view argues that economic recession is caused by interference with the free market mechanism — for example, minimum wage legislation, trade protectionism, inflation (which, it is argued, is always caused by governments printing too much money) and regulations of the activities of companies. Development, on the other hand, will be achieved by the LDCs if they adopt those measures necessary to attract foreign capital and to improve their competitiveness in the world market.

While it is argued that the operation of market forces is politically neutral (and this is the basis of the IMF's claim to neutrality), it is clear that this view of the world favours those who stand to gain from successfully competing in the open market, notably the owners of the transnational corporations and the international banks, whose funds are sought by LDCs in their efforts to improve their competitiveness.

However, this view of the world is rejected by those who argue that unregulated market forces give rise to periodic booms and slumps, illustrated precisely by the lack of regulation in the international loan market that led to the 1982 debt crisis. Market forces need to be managed, it is argued, so that booms and slumps can be mitigated or avoided by judicious government intervention. There is a wide range of views as to the degree and type of economic management required, but this view would recognise that, for development to occur in the LDCs, some form of government controls are necessary. These could range from providing concessionary lending to certain sectors of the economy, import regulations, regulations on the operations of foreign companies and even the nationalisation of certain industries. If indeed it is poor or insufficient management that is the cause of recession, then it is up to the IMF to intervene more forcefully if that process is to be reversed.

A third economic viewpoint argues that the above efforts at economic management are merely the attempts of those who benefit from an inherently unjust world order to patch it up and avoid the obvious conclusion that economic slumps are an inherent part of the profit maximising behaviour of those who control the system. This view argues that the private ownership of productive resources concentrates wealth in a few hands and therefore creates poverty for the majority. The only solution is a system of economic planning and control, operated by and on behalf of the poorest sections of the population, that would protect them against the power of those who accumulated the wealth created by the efforts of the poor themselves. This will only be achieved by radical social changes in every country. The *status quo* cannot be reformed, least of all by those who benefit from the present situation. This economic view of the world would serve the interests of those groups of people currently excluded from participating in the benefits of economic development. This would certainly include the majority of the population of the LDCs.

Where Does the IMF Stand?

It is clear that the IMF tends to accept the first of the three economic viewpoints outlined. Its operations illustrate its rejection of any notion of LDCs protecting their industry or direct government planning and control in the economy, in favour of the unfettered operation of market forces. Direct state intervention is seen as hindering the successful operation of the free market. The Fund favours the use of deflation and then devaluation, rather than direct controls over trade as a means of limiting imports, and assumes that growth will always take place where governments give private enterprise the freedom to make profitable investments.

The IMF's belief in automatic adjustment by the market has led it to assume that, if all countries were to observe these basic rules, there must ensue a 'natural' tendency for all balance of payments to remain in equilibrium over time. Thus it was assumed that countries which were in surplus for a few years would find that their costs of production were rising because of the necessity to increase wages and imports of raw materials and other inputs, while those in deficit would be able to keep their costs low because their industries would be expanding less rapidly. This would lead to a reduction in exports from the successful country and an expansion of those from the unsuccessful one, with a corresponding tendency for surpluses and deficits to be reversed. No direct government intervention would be required to bring about this change. So the role of the international monetary agency would be merely to ensure that all the countries involved observed the rules in order to make it possible for this process to take its 'natural' course.

In these circumstances, countries would find it relatively easy to maintain currency convertibility and exchange rate stability and they would rarely require any significant amount of balance of payments assistance. Yet it was recognised that short-term problems could arise which might create such a need. Poor weather conditions might lead to a bad harvest and the need for large increases in food imports; a sudden decline in the price of exported raw materials might lead to a drop in export earnings. In these circumstances a country would face a 'temporary disequilibrium' of its balance of payments and be tempted to use protectionist measures if some form of short-term credit were not available. Thus the IMF saw its power to lend as a means to overcome these short-term difficulties, rather than as a means to solve a long-term problem resulting from the fact that certain economies were internationally less competitive than others and therefore in need of long-term assistance in order to be able to survive and expand.

Most theorists did accept that LDCs would need long-term international credit in order to finance their industrialisation programmes. This, however, was defined as a 'developmental' as opposed to a 'monetary' need and it was to be provided by the World Bank (which, like the IMF, was established at the Bretton Woods conference of 1944), the private banks and the multinational firms. Thus, when an IMF team visits a country in order to negotiate a stand-by arrangement, its primary concern is to reduce the balance of payments deficit within a relatively short period of time (usually with in three to five years). The team assumes that direct state intervention is not necessary for the objective to be achieved and that the balance of payments problem is caused by high local inflation, which is itself caused by high government spending (funded by a large supply of new money), which leads to high levels of local consumption in relation to the level of output of goods which can be sold abroad. Given these assumptions, such a team tends to require policies which emphasise reductions in consumption rather than an increase in production. It justifies its position by the fact that a country with a balance of payments deficit is consuming more than it is producing. It does this by importing more goods than it is exporting. Unless such a country can obtain continuing supplies of international credit or aid for this process, it must eventually come to an end.

Further, the IMF also argues that the money it lends to a country makes that country able to continue to import for longer than would have been the case if IMF loans were not available. Without the IMF, it claims, abrupt cuts in spending and investment would have to be made to reduce the deficit. IMF assistance allows debtor countries to adopt policies that lead to a more gradual reduction in the deficit. Thus, some people would argue that the existence of the IMF makes possible a higher level of economic activity for deficit countries, especially when it is realised that the negotiation of an IMF agreement usually enables the country to also borrow extensively from the private banks.

Given the absence of alternative means of providing assistance to LDCs on a concessional basis (and it is well known that the levels of aid are now running at less than half the amount recommended by the Pearson Commission in the 1960s), these arguments must have some validity. However, it is also important to recognise that the negotiation of a stand-by arrangement with the IMF (a so-called 'stabilisation programme') does involve the country in the acceptance of a particular kind of policy and one which directly contradicts the policies which many of the more radical Third World governments were trying to implement in the 1950s and 1960s.

Policy Implications

Although the IMF conducts all of its negotiations individually and attempts to design programmes to fit the particular needs of each country, its programmes have a number of common features. Firstly, there is a general assumption that excessive expenditure by the state, particularly where this takes the form of encouraging higher levels of consumption rather than production, should be reduced. Thus the fund will attempt to cut levels of government borrowing and this, by implication, will mean a corresponding cut in the services provided by the state. In countries with more reactionary governments this can mean an attempt by the IMF to limit the exploitation of the state by corrupt and incompetent politicians, civil servants and business people; in more progressive countries, such as Jamaica under the Manley government, it will mean a reduction in welfare services for the poor. Subsidies to loss-making nationalised industries will also be subject to pressure and it is not unusual for the IMF to recommend that such industries be sold off to private enterprise. Furthermore, there is likely to be pressure to reduce state subsidies on the price of either consumer goods or inputs for uncompetitive industries.

Second, associated with this attack on state spending will be an attempt either to reduce wages or to limit their growth to less than the growth in productivity in industry. Rising wages make it difficult for local producers to compete effectively abroad and therefore to export successfully. Rising wages are also said to generate an increase in consumption, which can only be met through imports since local production cannot usually expand rapidly enough to meet the increased demand.

Third, while it is assumed that these cuts in wages and services will reduce imports, it is also assumed that they will lead to an increase in the profits of the private sector, since private capitalists will subsequently have to pay lower taxes and reduced labour costs. This will make it possible for both domestic and foreign capital to increase their investment in productive capacity and thereby either reduce the need for imports or increase the overall level of production in the long run. In this respect, an increase in the activities of foreign capital is thought to be especially useful because the capital which they import, as well as the goods which they produce, serves to reduce the level of the balance of payments deficit.

Last, the IMF will tend to discourage the use of direct controls over trade to reduce the deficit. It is very likely to demand a devaluation of the currency and will also try to do away with all attempts to use the rate of exchange to favour local as opposed to foreign producers. Although the Fund will not insist on the elimination of tariffs, it will probably resist any attempt to increase them and might even attempt to have them reduced. Thus it will be forcing the country concerned to secure the improvement in its trade by increasing the competitiveness of its goods, rather than by using direct controls to favour local over foreign producers.

Do IMF Policies Work?

In order to evaluate the role of the IMF, we must consider more than merely its own view of the effects of its operations. We have also to consider the extent to which its beliefs and the operation of the international monetary economy actually work in practice and the extent to which the Fund's programmes attack the underlying causes of chronic balance of payments deficits.

We have noted that the economic theory adopted by the IMF assumes that there will be a natural tendency for countries to maintain a long-term balance of payments equilibrium, provided that they do not interfere with the 'natural' operation of the market mechanism. Thus countries are supposed to achieve a balance between surplus and deficit over time, with a continuous growth in trade leading to a continuous improvement in the productivity and efficiency of the world economy.

But, when we look at the world during the post-war period, we find that matters have turned out differently. Some of the strong industrialised countries, notably West Germany and Japan, have been able to sustain more or less permanent balance of payments surpluses. Their foreign reserves have grown enormously and their capitalists have not invested a significant part of their surpluses abroad. Their very competitive exports are constantly taking over foreign markets especially in the LDCs. They are even more competitive in their home market, so that few foreign producers can increase their sales by exporting to them. Their tendency to save rather than spend their foreign surplus, together with their ability to compete more effectively than everyone else leads to deflation in those countries which cannot find expanding markets elsewhere. This growth in the strong countries does expand the market for raw materials, but it inhibits the growth of manufacturing in weaker countries, which many people believe is the only means to create a balanced growth process.

Two of the leading industrial countries, the US and Britain, have been in almost permanent deficit since the war. The fact that the US ran this deficit after the war was largely responsible for the ability of the strong countries to grow so rapidly. Marshall aid and defence spending by the US provided both capital and markets for European and Japanese industry. However, the continuation and growth of the deficit now leads to high interest rates, which have led to an inevitable reduction in the level of international demand. This will make it even more difficult for expansion to take place in those countries which had relied on exporting to the US.

If we look at the Third World, on the other hand, we find a more or less permanent tendency to balance of payments deficit. A few countries, such as Taiwan, South Korea, Hong Kong and Singapore, have been able to maintain high growth rates by increasing their industrial exports. Another small group, notably the oil exporters, have been able to capitalise on high prices for raw materials. All of these countries have been able to sustain very rapid rates of growth, especially from the late 1960s through to the late 1970s. On the other

36

hand, less fortunate LDCs, and these include the great bulk of the world's population outside the Communist bloc, have been faced with more or less permanent deficits.

While world trade was expanding very rapidly from the late 1940s to the early 1970s, even these most disadvantaged countries were able to maintain reasonable growth rates, albeit at the expense of increasing levels of economic inequality. But the intensification of the world economic crisis after 1974, coupled with concurrent oil price rises, left these countries facing massive deficits which could only be controlled through drastic cuts in living standards and in the level of economic activity. Although this problem was precipitated by the oil price rise, this was not its only cause. The real price of oil declined continuously until 1978, as did the surpluses of OPEC members, but the Third World deficit failed to go away as the surpluses of the strong industrial countries increased. The more recent increases in oil prices in 1979-80, stemming from the reduction in Iranian output, greatly intensified the problem, pushing West Germany and Japan into deficit and making it virtually impossible for the Third World as a whole to maintain even its reduced level of imports.

The combined deficit of these countries reached US$88 billion in 1981. Thus the real situation faced by these countries is not one in which the implementation of a few cuts in wages and services will restore the equilibrium while leaving the country undamaged. It is one in which restoring the equilibrium will require such massive cuts that all aspects of economic progress will be affected. Thus, the idea of a system that adjusts 'naturally', automatically balancing deficits and surpluses between countries, does not measure up to what really happens. Chronic deficits and permanent surpluses have characterised post-war development.

Do IMF Policies Resolve Chronic Deficits?

In the face of this chronic situation, the IMF has devised policies to reduce deficits to manageable proportions. We must now ask if such policies, designed to alleviate short-term problems, actually confront the underlying causes of chronic deficit.

On the whole, IMF programmes have succeeded in meeting their primary objective, the reduction in the short term balance of payments deficit. But they do this at very substantial cost in terms of reduced consumption, damage to local industry and increased inequality. Given the need to solve the problem quickly, most of the improvements have to be secured through a reduction in domestic consumption rather than an increase in production for export or in import substitution. The overall effect is therefore likely to be deflationary, involving a decline in the overall level of economic activity and a corresponding reduction in both local consumption and in long-term economic progress.

During periods when the world economy is expanding, the effects of such a programme might not be too severe, since the country might well be able to resume its growth rate once it had made the necessary adjustments. When, on the other hand, conditions are depressed, the results are likely to be much less favourable. In present conditions, which are worse than any since the 1930s, the results of such an approach can be disastrous.

First, in trying to increase their exports, the LDCs immediately confront the strong capitalist countries, which are attempting to do exactly the same. However, the latter have the advantage of producing on a very large scale, selling to a huge home market as well as having established markets abroad, having direct use of highly-trained workforces and sophisticated research facilities and having a monopoly over many areas of technology and skills. Given all of these factors, the possibility of competing with them on equal terms is almost negligible.

The only 'advantage' that most LDCs have over these established producers is the very low wages which their workers can be paid. Even this, however, is of relatively limited value. On the one hand, the existence of low wages means that local markets are very small, thus making it difficult to produce on a sufficiently large scale to reap the full advantage of modern production methods. On the other, low-paid workers tend to be poorly trained and motivated, so their productivity is correspondingly low. Furthermore, the advanced countries have been able continuously to adopt new technology (the automation secured through the micro-chip is only the most recent example), which has enabled them to pay much higher wages to their workers and still produce goods more cheaply than the average Third World producer.

In sectors such as cotton textiles, where cheap labour does provide low-wage countries with international competitive advantages, the industrialised countries have tended to ignore their professed belief in free trade and have adopted protective controls in order to defend jobs and capital investment in that sector. Thus by reducing tariff protection in their home markets and attempting to grow by exporting manufactures, LDCs render themselves very vulnerable. Several countries have found that established industries in their own countries have been destroyed as a result of tariff barriers having been lowered.

Second, the reduction of state spending, while it might enable producers to pay lower taxes, will also have the effect of reducing domestic demand for their products. Thus, producers will lose some of their home market (this market is usually the most profitable for them) and this loss of demand may mean a reduction in total production. Such a reduction will inevitably mean that the costs of producing each unit of output will rise as fixed costs (those that do not vary with the level of a company's production, factory rent for example) will have to be offset by a smaller total production. This will lead to increased selling prices and therefore the firm will be less competitive internationally. Nor will the lower taxes necessarily encourage producers to invest their increased wealth in local industry. When demand is being reduced through the reduction in wages and government spending, they are more likely to spend it on consumer goods (which are very likely to be imported), or invest it abroad. The latter is most likely to happen where a significant portion of local production is already in the hands of foreign capitalists who find it very easy to remove their profits from LDCs, either directly through legal channels or indirectly by various forms of transfer pricing. Thus, unless the reductions in wages and other costs are very large and the opportunity for increasing export markets very favourable, deflationary policies are quite likely to lead to a cut in a society's consumption and productivity, without leading to a subsequent improvement.

Third, while the effects of these policies might be positive with respect to individual countries' balance of payments deficits, their effects on the overall world economy are likely to be very harmful. At the moment, a few OPEC countries, together with one or two of the most successful industrialised countries, have balance of payments surpluses. The rest of the developed world and nearly all the oil importing LDCs are now trying to overcome their deficits by cutting imports and increasing exports. But, since most of their potential customers are attempting to do the same, the result can only be intensified competition, in which the most powerful might succeed, but at the expense of the weaker nations. It is clearly impossible for all countries to increase exports and reduce imports at the same time.

In this situation, it is suggested that the few surplus countries should increase their imports and reduce their foreign reserves. But this is highly unlikely to occur. The bulk of these surpluses are in the hands of small Middle Eastern countries. What they do is to lend their surpluses to the international banks, which then lend them to deficit countries. This, however, has the long-term effect of increasing levels of indebtedness of the deficit countries. This means they will have higher interest and capital repayment commitments and will therefore have less resources available to develop their own industrial base. Thus, their ability to generate exportable production and improve their balance of payments, will be hindered. Again, we find a short-term solution being adopted which must worsen the problem in the long run.

The present debt crisis means that many LDCs are so heavily indebted that they can scarcely borrow enough to service their existing debts. Despite debt renegotiations, the present burden of debt servicing makes growth a remote prospect. The possibility that a recession in the LDCs, inspired by debt, could truncate the present tentative upswing in the developed countries has not been discounted. The summit meeting at Williamsburg in the US, in May 1983, offered little hope of world recovery to stimulate struggling LDC economies.

The Paradoxical Mechanism of Feedback from the External Debt

For the oil-importing developing countries, the large disequilibria in the balance of payments on current accounts, aggravated by the impact of the crisis on their exports, the worsening of the terms of trade and the rise in interest rates, were expressed in an annual deficit that rose to around US$80 billion in 1979 and 1980, greatly surpassed US$90 billion in 1981 and continued to rise in 1982. The result of all this was the rapid increase in their external debts, which, depending on the method of calculation that is used, are now approaching or have surpassed US$600 billion. This debt, whose magnitude was first determined by the need to obtain resources with which to pay for the deficits in their current accounts, has, with time, become a factor adding to the deficit and, in fact, a feedback mechanism that takes an increasing toll of the product of people's work, more than a third of which goes to the transnational banks.

This may be proved with data from the World Bank, according to which debt servicing took US$99 billion (85 per cent) of the US$117 billion obtained as loans by the underdeveloped countries in 1981, leaving a net transfer of resources of only US$18 billion (US$600 million in the case of Latin America). Things have come to such an extreme that the underdeveloped countries are incurring new debts practically for the sole purpose of meeting the obligations created by their own indebtedness. Such an absurd, perverted, irrational phenomenon as this is unprecedented in the history of international economic relations.

Report to Seventh Summit Conference of the Non-aligned Countries (1983), page 90.

Last, although the IMF always presents its policies as non-political, and based entirely on scientific economic theory, there can be no doubt that their recommendations correspond to the policies favoured by large-scale international capital and its supporters in Third World countries. It is the strong multinational companies which have most to gain from policies which favour the free movement of goods and money, since they are able to move their investments to whichever country offers them the greatest concessions and therefore, profit potential. Many of the individuals involved in local political activities depend for their own political and economic privileges on their links with these corporations and with the governments of the main world

---

US Treasury denies bias on IMF loans

The US Treasury yesterday disputed reports that it had frequently sought to influence decisions by the International Monetary Fund on the basis of political judgment. 'This was a misrepresentation', an official said.

The issue is extremely sensitive because of an effort in Congress to attach new conditions to the US contribution to the IMF's quota increase, which would prevent future loans to the apartheid regime in South Africa.

A report prepared for the House Foreign Affairs Sub-committee by the Congressional Research Service said that on a number of occasions the US may have sought to influence loans for political reasons. One version of the report, which was obtained by *The Wall Street Journal,* says there has been a 'hit list' of countries regarded as not deserving aid.

According to the report, the former Secretary of State, Mr Alexander Haig, ruled at one point that the left leaning government of Grenada should not 'get a penny of indirect aid' from the IMF and other multinational institutions. Countries said to be on the hit list include Vietnam, Cuba, Afghanistan, Nicaragua and Grenada, all of which are assumed by the US to be under the influence of the Soviet Union.

Chile was alleged to have been on the list when the Marxist Allende Government was in power in the 1970s and Laos, Cambodia, Mozambique and Uganda are said to have been put on the list by the Carter administration as part of an effort to get funding from Congress.

Guardian, 19 May 1983.

powers which lie behind them. Many such multinational corporations use their economic power and political leverage to force countries to seek IMF assistance and submit to its conditions. Furthermore, the powerful western members of the IMF have used access to the Fund's resources as an instrument of their own foreign policy objectives. This has been clearly demonstrated in the case of the US reaction to requests for IMF assistance from the different Central American countries. (See box page 44).

If debtor nations accept assistance from the IMF, they must accept the conditions that accompany that assistance. The case studies in this book illustrate the implications of these conditions for the majority of the population in the countries concerned and show how, even within their own terms, IMF policies failed to solve the crises they were intended to confront.

In the case of Jamaica, Winston James examines the relationship between the IMF and the 'democratic socialist' government of Michael Manley. The study shows the problems which face a Third World government committed to reform. Manley was first elected prime minister in 1972 and re-elected in 1976 on a wave of popular support under the banner 'Better must come'. But his government was marked by a massive fall in the living standards of the urban and rural poor, precisely those sectors which had voted for him. The Manley government effectively abandoned its commitment to reform when it agreed to implement IMF austerity measures. But it is also clear that Manley was caught in a political contradiction of his own making. On the one hand, he attempted to appease his popular base through radical rhetoric while on the other he tried to appeal to Jamaica's private sector to collaborate with him. Jamaica's businessmen were alarmed by the rhetoric and they refused to co-operate with the government. Instead they sabotaged its efforts through a virtual investment strike and capital flight. Manley was left with two alternatives, to radicalise his programme toward structural changes in the economy which would involve a confrontation with Jamaica's business and landowning class or to capitulate to IMF policies which essentially favoured that class and fell most heavily on his own political base. Manley opted for the latter and in the process paved the way for his own massive election defeat in 1980.

The irony was that not only did IMF policies conflict with Manley's own programme of reforms, but they did not actually work. The Jamaican experience shows the inadequacy of IMF policies even within their own terms. Despite the sacrifices they implied for the majority of the Jamaican people, they failed to solve the crisis of the Jamaican economy, precisely because their analysis of the problem, rising imports and falling exports caused by excessive wage rises, proved to be incorrect.

The relationship between the IMF and Manley's successor Edward Seaga illustrates the failure of the IMF policies even more clearly. Seaga has never made even a verbal commitment to reform, but has a personal and ideological commitment to the IMF 'view of the world'. His willingness to accept IMF medicine, and in turn the IMF's commitment to give Seaga immeasurably more favourable treatment than it gave to Manley, is a good test of the effectiveness of its policies. In fact, Jamaica has plunged deeper into crisis. Bauxite production has fallen, the currency has been effectively devalued, wages have been reduced by 10 per cent since 1980 and unemployment has risen over 40 per cent among some sectors of the workforce.

The experience of Chile under the government of General Augusto Pinochet is another example of the failure of the IMF policies to work, despite their implementation by a government ideologically attuned to the IMF's economic view. Pinochet came to power in 1973 through a coup which overthrew the democratically elected Marxist government of Salvador Allende. Pinochet collaborated closely with the monetarist economic technocrats known as the Chicago Boys and pursued policies which went beyond any shock treatment which the IMF had ever dared to impose. This could happen in Chile because its repressive military government ensured that popular opposition to these policies were stifled. The IMF facilitated the monetarist experiment by giving the Pinochet government its seal of approval in 1975, which subsequently enabled the regime to obtain the loans from the private international banks which were needed to sustain the model. The total collapse by 1981 of the monetarist experiment in Chile is a salutary lesson in the failure of IMF prescriptions, even when applied in their most rigorous form and by a government totally committed to their success.

The case of Peru highlights the importance of the IMF as police officer of the international economy. The private banks attempted to impose their own conditions on Peru in return for a loan agreement. When they discovered that they lacked the authority to ensure that these conditions were fulfilled, they withdrew, forcing the Peruvian government to turn to the IMF, which does have the power to impose such conditions.

The Peruvian case, like that of Jamaica and Chile, illustrates the tremendous social cost that IMF policies bring with them. The Peruvian crisis was only temporarily halted when world prices for its exports rose briefly at the end of the 1970s. The collapse of these prices in the 1980s put the country once again into the hands of the IMF under the government of President Fernando Belaúnde. In the meantime, the lives of the country's poor have steadily worsened. In

1983, *Time* magazine spoke of a psychological study of 100 school children from a Lima shantytown. No fewer than 60 per cent of them had learning disabilities caused by malnutrition: 'In Peru, chronic malnutrition and disease threaten to rob the country of an entire generation of its young', *Time* concluded.

These three case studies give important insights into the present crisis facing Third World nations. As successive governments are forced to turn to the IMF for assistance in the face of their enormous debt burdens and balance of payments difficulties, the experiences of Jamaica, Chile and Peru are being repeated. IMF programmes are not solving the structural balance of payments problems that debtor nations face, the high social costs of IMF restructuring are still being paid by the poorest sections of the population and draconian austerity measures are provoking political confrontation which in some cases, notably Brazil (see box page 9) may have far-reaching consequences.

Growing social unrest, in the form of spontaneous riots or organised opposition by workers in key economic sectors, has an explosive political potential in Latin America and elsewhere in the Third World. Ironically, the IMF may find that, in imposing its conditions, it creates a social and political explosion which threatens the stability of the countries concerned and makes it even less likely that governments will repay their debts. Third World governments have to consider this risk, particularly in the light of the IMF's sorry record in solving their economic problems.

The lesson of Michael Manley's democratic socialism in Jamaica may have the most relevance to the crisis of the Third World. For Jamaica raised once again the key question of whether limited reforms in Third World countries can really solve the problems of the Third World majority. By opposing reform-oriented governments but failing to provide solutions through its conservative, free market recipes, the IMF may well be paving the way for more radical solutions, which have implications not only for internal power structures but also for the international economy.

Central America: The Financial War

Not all the war is in the jungles. Since 1981 the Reagan administration has fought a bitter campaign in the boardrooms of Washington to make the international financial institutions cut off

▶

---

their loans to Nicaragua and multiply aid to El Salvador and Guatemala instead. By 1983 the campaign had largely succeeded.

El Salvador

The story begins in July 1981 when El Salvador applied for US$36 million from the IMF's Compensatory Financing Facility. On July 27, the executive board, consisting of representatives of the Fund's member countries, met to consider the loan. J.J. Polak, executive director for the Netherlands, was the first to speak.

His speech was a shocker. He contended not only that the loan was ill-advised but that it would violate IMF rules. The IMF's technical staff had refused to recommend the loan for adoption and never had the Fund approved any loan without the concurrence of the staff. The particular loan facility to which El Salvador was applying had very clear technical rules which the IMF had scrupulously adhered to in all cases. The right to borrow from the Compensatory Financing Facility hinged on a forecast of a country's future export earnings, a forecast that would demonstrate (1) that the country was suffering from an export shortfall and (2) that the shortfall was temporary. The staff had concluded that conditions were too unsettled in El Salvador to permit a realistic projection of future exports and rather than make up imaginary numbers had declined to make any projection at all. But access to the facility was not allowed without the forecast. Without it there was no way to determine whether the shortfall was temporary.

Therefore, Polak told the executive board, routine approval of the loan could have 'important — I would say serious — consequences for the Fund's relations with its members and for the Fund's conditionality'. He warned the board that the IMF 'has a long and unbroken tradition that the Board discusses requested transactions only on the basis of a staff paper that seeks to establish the validity of the request in the light of the Fund's policies. Even a single deviation from that principle would set a serious precedent.'

This authoritative speech made it clear that approval of the loan would violate the IMF's rules. J.J. Polak was formerly director of research for the IMF in charge of preparing the commodity forecasts for the compensatory financing facility. No one was better schooled in the rules and precedents.

Executive board discussion

In the discussion that followed the West European members of the IMF, except Italy, opposed the loan on the grounds that it broke the rules. The Third World members supported it, sometimes with reservations, because of the basic North-South division in the Fund. The Third World members always press for easier conditions on

♦

Fund loans, whether compensatory or standby. The US director, Richard Erb, despite numerous directives from the Reagan administration to tighten the conditionality of IMF loans, in this case supported the loan.

British position

Speaking for Great Britain, Lionel Price said he did not think the request met the requirements for the contemporary financing facility. Paragraph six of Decision No.6224 set out clearly the basis on which the Fund would establish that the member had an export shortfall of a short-term character. In particular, it was necessary to establish a forecast for exports in the two post-shortfall years, something that had not been done in the present case.

If data supporting El Salvador's case became available, he could support the loan, Price continued. But as of now, it seemed to him 'that the request had been presented to the Executive Board without essential information'. He abstained.

US position

US executive director Richard Erb acknowledged that other executive directors felt the United States was pressing the Fund to bring the El Salvador loan to the executive board and that newspaper articles had left the impression that the US was planning to use the IMF to serve specific national political objectives in Central America. He insisted that 'in fact, the exact opposite was intended by his Government'. The United States valued the IMF's economic surveillance and adjustment programmes. Both the government and Congress had a conviction that the IMF should not be used to serve more specific US political and security objectives. The United States had 'in no way pressed the management of the Fund in the case of El Salvador'. Erb sharply criticised the IMF's management for not coming up with the export projections needed to justify the loan. The management should have known that international coffee prices, not internal conditions, were the reason for the shortfall. In the shortfall year itself, Erb argued, that was clearly the case. By not making a forecast for the post-shortfall years the management was implying that the internal situation would become much worse and that the cause of the shortfall in 1982 and 1983 would be internal developments, Erb argued.

In short, the staff have erred, the United States contended. Thus executive director Erb implicitly adopted a double standard. When the staff concurred with US desires, then 'technical' formulae reigned supreme. But when the staff's interpretation of those formulae differed from the US position, then the staff was in error

➤

and the United States was free to interpret the formulae to suit its desires.

Erb seemed unaware that this was a precedent that other nations could follow as well.

The United States, with 19 per cent of the vote, plus Canada, Italy, and the Third World directors who spoke comprised 57 per cent of the vote and the loan passed. It takes a simple majority to pass a loan.

The 1981 loan decision was the most hotly contested in the IMF's history up to that time, surpassed only by the 3 November 1982 argument over the loan to South Africa. It was without precedent for a loan to be railroaded through over the protests of so many important member countries. For the US had indeed pushed the loan through. Although US executive director Erb was correct in saying that his government values the general surveillance and adjustment programmes of the IMF, he misled the board and later Congress, in denying that the United States was pressing the IMF in the specific case of el Salvador. Had such a weak case been presented by some leftist country the US administration felt strongly about, whether Grenada, Nicaragua, Vietnam, Madagascar, or even India, the United States would have stressed the technical grounds against a loan. In fact it did oppose the loan applications of all these countries in the IMF or other international financial institutions. But when El Salvador applied with its technically shaky case, the US dropped its usual insistence on strict interpretation of the rules.

Nicaragua

In the spring of 1979, as Nicaragua was convulsed in civil war, the Sandinistas implored the IMF not to make a planned loan of US$60 million to Somoza. The money would all go into Somoza's pockets, they said, yet would add to the national debt which the new government would inherit. In the United States, church and human rights groups went directly to Secretary of the Treasury Michael Blumenthal and asked for the same thing. The IMF made the loan anyway, just nine weeks before Somoza's overthrow. As predicted, when the new government's financial experts took over they found that Somoza had completely cleaned out the central bank.

But that was not all. Under the IMF's Compensatory Financing Facility, a member nation is allowed to offer estimates for the last few months of the claimed shortfal year it those last few months follow the date of the loan application. However, if the estimates turn out to be wrong, the country is required to repay the loan immediately. Sure enough, Somoza's concocted estimated were way off and in September 1979 the new Sandinista government was

▶

required to pay back immediately the money Somoza had spirited away.

That was enough for the Nicaraguans. The Sandinistas decided to exclude the IMF from their delicate negotiations on rescheduling the Somoza-era debt, for which the new government took full responsibility. They declined to submit to the onerous conditions the IMF would have imposed for any stand-by agreement because these would conflict with the government's proposed positive income redistribution and plans for reflating the economy. As a result, the IMF has contributed nothing to Nicaragua's reconstruction. The IMF's loan to Somoza has been one of the most ill-advised in the IMF's 35-year history and the Fund was lucky the successor government assumed responsibility for it at all.

The upshot of the Fund's inflexibility and the Sandinista's aloofness is that Nicaragua is deprived of the approximately US$200-300 million it is entitled to as a member of the IMF. As the Central American crisis deepens, IMF money is going to every country on the isthmus except Nicaragua.

International Policy Report, March 1983, published by the Centre for International Policy, USA.

4 The IMF and Monetarism in Chile

Since 1973, Chile has been the subject of widespread international attention out of all proportion to its weight in world affairs. Flagrant and systematic violations of human rights by the military regime of General Augusto Pinochet have done much to attract such interest. But the regime has also drawn unprecedented flak and fanfare for its radical experiment in economics. During the past 10 years, Chile has been a laboratory for those conservative monetarist theories, backed by the International Monetary Fund, which have been fashionable throughout the West.

Until recently, Chile's Chicago Boys — the group of Chilean economists who studied under free enterprise champion, Milton Friedman, at the University of Chicago, and who became Pinochet's economic architects — claimed miracle status for their policies. They pointed to the high rates of economic growth achieved by their economic model towards the end of the 1970s and to their success in reducing the annual rate of inflation from more than 500 per cent during the previous government to less than 10 per cent eight years later. They noted the triumphal advance of monetarism in other Latin American dictatorships and even in industrialised countries such as Britain and the US. They enjoyed the respect of the Reagan Administration's economic theorists, who praised Chile as a proof of the viability of supply-side economics and 'bite-the-bullet' government policies. When starting a further nine-year term on 11

March 1981, Pinochet declared: 'Seven years ago, we were alone in the world with . . . our determined advocacy of social market economy, in distinction to the socialising statism that dominated the western World . . . Today, we are part of a world-wide categorical trend. And I tell you, gentlemen, it is not Chile that has changed its mind'.

But today, Chile has lost its miracle status. A severe recession has deeply dented Pinochet's historical righteousness and some of the conceptual pillars of the economic model have now fallen. But the Chicago Boys' experiment in Chile remains a classic case study of the application of monetarism. Monetarists themselves have held Chile as the purest example and, therefore, the best testing ground of their theories. When confronted with the results of their policies in democratic countries, monetarists often claim that the prescribed medicine has not been properly applied because governments are too fearful of the electoral consequences. But the Chilean dictatorship has had no such qualms. It has applied monetarism rigorously, its freedom to experiment guaranteed by the brutal actions of the military in repressing the freedom of the Chilean people.

Like most underdeveloped countries, Chile is dependent on the receipt of external finance from foreign governments, private banks and international institutions. And, as in many other underdeveloped countries, the role of the IMF has been crucial and, at times, determinant. At one stage, in 1974 and 1975, the Fund directly influenced the design of the Chilean economic system; at a later stage the IMF supplied indirect but important support for the regime's policies by endorsing them before donor governments, aid institutions and private bankers. The Chilean model, therefore, in its rigid adherence to monetarism and to IMF philosophies, is a unique litmus test of the policies and perspectives which the IMF has pressed on all Third World governments seeking its financial support and seal of approval.

Inheritance and Legacy: The Allende Government

When Salvador Allende was inaugurated as the world's first freely-elected Marxist head of state on 4 November 1970, he inherited a country in profound economic and political crisis. For two decades, the rate of economic growth in Chile had languished well below the average for Latin America. The agricultural sector, riddled with inequalities in land ownership, had failed to produce the food required to support the growing urban population. Manufacturing had expanded sluggishly, failing to generate substantial employment and geared mostly to an elite market. Income distribution was highly

50

unequal: the average income of the top 1 per cent of the Chilean population was nine times that of the bottom 10 per cent and 72 per cent of the population received less than the national average wage. Government budget deficits and deficits in the balance of payments had become a way of life. External dependence was increasing rather than decreasing. Allende inherited a foreign debt of US$3 billion from his predecessor, with large debt service payments due in the early 1970s. Inflation had become endemic, with price increases averaging 26 per cent during the second half of the 1960s.

Allende's economic policies were a radicalisation of the changes initiated under the previous government of President Eduardo Frei, rather than a total break with the past. His immediate concern was to capitalise on his electoral victory by pushing through a number of fundamental changes as quickly as possible. Within the first year, foreign copper corporations were nationalised without compensation, having already been paid, it was argued, by the excess profits they had made over the years. The iron, nitrate and coal industries were also nationalised and a large part of manufacturing, as well as most of the banking system, were brought under state control. Land reform was rapidly accelerated. There was a redistribution of income as differential wage increases were decreed, while prices were controlled. In one year, salary and wage-earners saw their share of the national income jump from 51 to 59 per cent. There was also a huge expansion of education and housing programmes for the mass of the population.

During his first full year in office, Allende was able to claim a considerable degree of success by conventional standards. Idle capacity in the productive sector was stimulated by demand from the expanded purchasing power of lower-income groups and by greater public expenditure, which promoted economic growth without overheating the economy. Real Gross National Product increased by 8.6 per cent, while inflation was held to 22.1 per cent. Employment grew substantially and the unemployment rate in the capital, Santiago, dropped from 8.3 to 3.8 per cent. Chile seemed to be demonstrating that it was possible to have a socialist revolution with bread and without blood.

But, by early 1972, Chile's political life had become sharply polarised. The economy had begun to flounder and economic output had declined. Capital investment fell, as both foreign and national investors boycotted the new regime. The government's fiscal deficit increased and the country's balance of payments deficit grew alarmingly as its income from copper exports plummeted. Consumer prices rose by 163 per cent in 1972 and soared to more than 500 per cent the following year, according to official statistics.

Because imports of many goods were reduced and for structural

51

reasons, Chile's own industry was unable to increase production quickly enough to meet the growing demand generated by higher wages, rationing and shortages ensued. This led to vigorous complaints by the middle classes and encouraged shopkeepers to raise their prices unofficially.

The Allende government's ability to manage this deteriorating situation was severely restricted by several economic and structural factors. During 1971 and 1972, Chile experienced a 20 per cent fall in the dollar price of copper, its main export. Combined with a 41 per cent increase in the price of agricultural imports, the result was a 50 per cent erosion in the terms of trade between copper exports and food imports. With the foreign debt draining precious foreign exchange and foreign exchange reserves themselves depleted and with foreign sources of credit drying up (due to the political opposition to the regime by most credit suppliers) Chile could not purchase the imports required to sustain and increase production. This devastating situation damaged the entire economy and left the government little room for manoeuvre.

But the economic crisis was fundamentally a *political* crisis. Both internal and external political forces impeded the government's ability to limit the impact of problems rooted in the structure of the economy and to correct the financial problems arising from its own policies.

On the external front, the US government had committed itself to a campaign of destabilisation. The aim was to create sufficient economic chaos to make it impossible for Allende to govern and to pave the way for a military coup. As early as September 1970, after Allende's election, but before his inauguration, President Richard Nixon of the US instructed Richard Helms, director of the Central Intelligence Agency (CIA) to 'make the economy scream'. The campaign quietly but effectively established an invisible blockade of Chile. Credits from US agencies and from Washington-based multilateral institutions were delayed or denied. Private banks refused to renew other credits. Because of fears of nationalisation foreign companies operating in Chile postponed new investments, while foreign suppliers delayed the delivery of spare parts required by industry. Copper companies, which had been expropriated without compensation, retaliated by legal harassment through the international courts, laying claim to shipments of Chilean copper. This international aggression, initiated first by Washington *before* Allende began to implement his programme, forced the government to make mobilisation of political support at home one of its highest priorities. By providing material gains for its supporters the government secured this political support, but at the expense of causing inflation.

OFFICIAL LENDING TO CHILE FROM WASHINGTON BASED
AGENCIES
(millions of US dollars)

	1968-70	1971-73	1974-76
US Government Agencies[1]	236	44	433
World Bank/Inter-American Development Bank	136	30	304

1. AID, PL480, Eximbank, Commodity Credit Corp., Housing Investment Guaranty.

Source: Laurence Whitehead, 'Inflation and Stabilisation in Chile 1970-77', in Rosemary Thorp and Laurence Whitehead (eds.), *Inflation and Stabilisation in Latin America* (Oxford: The Macmillan Press, 1979), p.73.

Also on the internal front, opponents of Allende, encouraged by Washington, badgered the government at every turn. Private capital stopped investing and cut production. It also promoted hoarding, black-marketeering, illegal capital transfers and widespread acts of economic sabotage, including the now-famous shopkeepers' and truck-drivers' strike. Allende's supporters had failed to win a majority of the seats in the Chilean Congress, so opposition parties were able to deny the government the use of some major instruments of economic management, including anti-inflationary devices such as legislation to curb the black market. Allende's coalition government also had to deal with divisions among its own supporters over the pace and direction of political change, a dynamic which diverted attention from the so-called battle of production.

By mid-1972, the executive branch of government had virtually lost control over the management of the economy. It should be recalled, however, that the Allende government had agreed to discuss a stabilisation programme with an IMF mission scheduled to visit Chile on 15 October 1973. How those negotiations would have turned out will never be known. Four minutes before noon on 11 September 1973, two Hunter Hawk jets streaked across the skies of Santiago for the first of eight bombing runs on the presidential palace. Within hours, as Allende lay dead in the burning palace, Pinochet stepped forward as leader of Chile's new military junta.

Adopting IMF Doctrine: The New Dogmatists

Hours after the news of Allende's death had reached New York, US corporations whose Chilean subsidiaries had been nationalised

53

indicated readiness to resume operations 'if (the new) government were receptive to investment'. The expectations of foreign capital were not disappointed. The military government quickly announced it would re-open the copper industry to foreign investment and 'would pursue liberal economic policies based on private enterprise'. The first economic management team assembled by Pinochet was largely comprised of officials whose views were closely compatible with international financial institutions such as the IMF. Pinochet was pointedly playing to the international market place.

On seizing power, the military junta took absolute control of state and country. Political parties were banned, Congress dissolved, national trade unions suspended and severe restrictions imposed on professional associations. Nearly all organised groups and forces which traditionally exercised influence over Chilean economic policies, and in particular, nationalist and progressive voices, were suspended or destroyed. As Sergio de Castro, the Minister of Finance, later admitted, political repression gave the government an open field for economic policy-making: it 'allowed the economic management team absolute independence in pursuing precisely the policies they wanted'. Allende, on the eve of the *coup d'état,* had been virtually unable to control spending, raise taxes, contract foreign loans, punish economic crimes and subversive strikes, or sack a single public employee. After 11 September, by contrast, all obstacles to the exercise of executive authority were erased.

But the new administration at first presented no coherent economic policy. During the first months after the coup, the regime laid more emphasis on denouncing the financial problems it had inherited than in defining even a short-term economic programme. The junta's uncertain approach to the task of economic stabilisation was due in part to its determination to consolidate the dictatorship, a process which was initially aided by the resumption of foreign credits and by a 70 per cent rise in export revenue due to a boom in copper prices. Some measures were adopted at the outset, however, to reduce the country's financial imbalances. These included a substantial devaluation and the freeing of a wide range of goods from price controls. At the same time, the junta moved to reduce inflation both by slashing public sector employment (with the exception of the military, which was expanded by 20 per cent between 1973 and 1974 and whose budget was almost doubled) and by reducing real wages through a deliberate understatement of the inflation figure by which wages were periodically adjusted.

Even though international capital was already predisposed to the new government, Chilean authorities bent over backwards to elicit international confidence in their policies. They publicly indicated their wish to enter into a stand-by agreement with the IMF in the Fund's upper credit tranches. The strict conditionality that accompanies such requests is usually avoided at all costs by Third World countries. But the junta wanted a high level of conditionality in order to obtain international financial support and to strengthen the government's domestic position for the adoption of draconian economic measures.

Discussions with an IMF mission began shortly after the military takeover. There were important initial disagreements between the mission and the Chilean economic team: the Chileans resisted IMF arguments for a further devaluation and also objected to the mission's insistence that real wages be further reduced in 1974. But the IMF's approach was accepted as the basis for Chile's stabilisation programme. The junta accepted ceilings on government spending so that the Fund's targets for reducing real wages would be met. The exchange rate policy and measures to reduce state subsidies for items of popular consumption were also shaped in accordance with Fund recommendations. However, the Fund did not seem to exert significant direct influence over structural changes undertaken by the regime. These measures, denationalisation of expropriated industries, the return of land to previous owners and the drastic liberalisation of trade and tariff policies, were much more Chilean initatives than those of the Fund.

On 15 January 1974, the Chilean government signed a stand-by agreement with the IMF. Despite the regime's desire for discipline from outside, the US$94 million credit only engaged Chile's first credit tranche in the IMF. Nevertheless, the IMF's 'seal of approval'. cleared the way for substantial inflows of loans during 1974. The credit blockade by Washington-based bilateral and multilateral agencies dissolved. And, with the solid backing of the IMF, Chile had no problem in rescheduling more than 95 per cent of its debt payments due for 1974 and 1975. The debt renegotiations provided Chile with substantial relief on its obligations, equivalent to US$560 million, more than 70 per cent of all the bilateral official aid received by Chile in 1974. Coincidentally, this amount nearly corresponded to the US$550 million in debt incurred by the junta to pay generous compensation to foreign companies nationalised under Allende.

Shock Treatment

By the end of 1974, the military junta was secure in its seizure of state power. But serious economic problems remained. Economic growth had recovered during the year, but inflation remained at more than 375 per cent, four times the target set by the IMF and the administration's freeing of prices had erased the effects of reductions in real wages and cuts in government spending. By the beginning of 1975, the external aspects of the economy were critical. With imports continuing to rise, the projected balance of payments deficit for 1975 was extremely high.

The government's prospects for obtaining credits from private banks to cover this deficit were bleak. With international capital markets very tight during 1975, private banks were favouring only their prime customers. Looking at Chile's expected balance of payments, aware of its low level of foreign exchange reserves and feeling less than confident in the political stability of the regime, private bankers still considered Chile a high-risk country and were only willing to commit limited amounts of capital.

Once again, the military government turned to official foreign aid sources, both bilateral and multilateral, for external finance. Another postponement of payments on its foreign debts was crucial. But, in 1975, renegotiations of the debt encountered opposition in the Paris Club. Before the creditors in the Club met, several governments, including those of Britain and Scandinavia, announced they would not attend the meeting because of the junta's gross violations of human rights. In these circumstances, the authorities felt obliged to sign another agreement with the IMF in order to argue better their case at the Paris Club. The Club even postponed its meeting officially to let negotiations between Chile and the IMF be completed first. Once a stand-by agreement had been signed, in March 1975, the Paris Club granted Chile debt relief of US$232 million, equivalent to about three-quarters of total bilateral aid received during 1975.

In this way, the IMF came to play a pivotal role in defining the course and content of Chilean economic policy. In an interview in *Euromoney* (July 1978), de Castro left little doubt about the determinant impact of the Fund's hard-line position in negotiations with Chile:

After the price of copper went down in '75 we projected a deficit in the balance of payments of US$1.2 billion. In conversations with the IMF, we were told we could not have a bigger deficit than US$50 million because we could not get financial support for more than that. After a lot of haggling, we came to an agreed deficit of US$240 million. The only way to do that was to cut down drastically.

The drastic cuts imposed by the Fund directly affected wages and government spending. Excessive demand was still blamed by the Fund experts for Chile's galloping inflation. Even though the government's own programme of wage restraints meant a reduction of real wages in 1975 and by the end of 1974, they were already 35 per cent less than their 1969 level, the Fund insisted on even lower real wages. On government spending, the Fund set rigid quarterly limits so that the authorities were forced to institute even more severe trimming in the government budget. The stand-by agreement reached between the IMF and Chile in March 1975 dipped into Chile's second and third credit tranches and consequently obliged Chile to respect the IMF's conditions.

However, the external influence of the Fund was not the sole determinant of a shift to more hard-line economics in 1975. A re-established economic elite was now secure enough to push ahead with stringent policies, consistent with its own view of a new economic order for Chile. Its members were prepared to disregard the domestic social consequences. By 1975, this entrepreneurial elite had grown increasingly critical of the limited and gradualist approach to economic management carried out in 1974. It gained very strong backing and encouragement by the visit, in March 1975, to Chile of two world-famous advocates of monetarist ultra-orthodoxy: Milton Friedman and Arnold Harberger of the Economics Department of the University of Chicago. Friedman impressed Pinochet with his clear-cut prescription for Chile's economic malaise:

The immediate cause of inflation is always a larger increase in the money supply than in output; this is clearly the Chilean case. The first need is to eliminate inflation and the only way in which Chile can finish with inflation is by eliminating drastically the fiscal deficit, preferably by reducing public expenditure . . . gradualism seems to me to be impossible.

To make a clear break with gradualism, as suggested by Friedman, the military junta named a new, more doctrinaire economic team in April 1975. Symbolic of the new team was Jorge Cauas, appointed Minister of Economics with a 'superminister' mandate to supervise all other economic ministries and government agencies. Trained at the University of Chicago and apprenticed as a high-ranking official of the World Bank, Cauas was well known in international financial circles, a qualification which facilitated his ability to negotiate the 1975 agreement with the IMF under difficult political circumstances. Men like Cauas, many of them also Chicago Boys, displaced members of the armed forces, career civil servants and economists linked to political parties (such as the National Party and the Christian Democrats) which had originally supported the *coup d'état*. 'We want only technical experts', Pinochet declared as he purged from government the last representatives of nationalist economic thinking.

In mid-April 1975, the new economic team announced the drastic austerity measures which became widely known as 'the shock treatment'. Following the IMF diagnosis that the ailment in Chile's economy was excessive demand, the authorities applied the Fund's recessionary remedy, a painful bleeding of the economy by intentionally contracting output. Public sector employment was frozen. Government spending was slashed with a one-third cut in subsidies to public enterprises and a two-thirds cut in government spending on housing and public works. Wage cuts suggested by the IMF were also implemented, resulting in a further decline in real incomes. And, in their zeal, the new dogmatists in charge of managing the economy went beyond IMF recommendations. They further reduced tariff protection for Chilean industries and generally moved towards opening the economy to foreign competition.

This shock treatment delivered a body-blow to the economy. The Gross Domestic Product decreased by 11 per cent. Industrial production plummeted by more than 25 per cent and capital investment fell below its already low levels. Small and medium-sized enterprises protested against the treatment which was sending many of them into bankruptcy. But it was the Chilean people who bore the brunt of the new measures. During 1975, real wages were almost 40 per cent less than their 1969 level and the share of wages and salaries in the national income fell from a high of 63 per cent in 1972 to 41 per cent in 1976. The biggest sacrifice was made by those who lost their jobs. Unemployment, which averaged 5 per cent in the 1960s and which had fallen to 3.1 per cent in 1972, grew dramatically to 9.2 per cent in 1974, 14.5 per cent in 1975 and peaked at 20 per cent in March 1976, according to official figures. The recession caused by the shock treatment was the worst for 45 years and the decline in output, 11.5 per cent, greatly surpassed the 3.6 per cent fall in output registered in 1973 immediately after the upheaval of the coup.

A December 1975 World Bank report glowed with satisfaction with the new Chilean economic model:

The Chilean government has made the hard policy decisions required, given its precarious balance of payments and international reserve positions and has met its international debt service obligations, while at the same time introducing certain fundamental reforms that lay the basis for resuming economic growth. It has gone a long way towards rationalising the public sector budgetary process and opening the domestic economy to the opportunities and competition of the world economy . . . These measures are consistent with the recommendations made repeatedly by the Bank and other international institutions over the past decade.

After describing in detail the government's economic goals and directions, the same report concluded categorically: 'These objectives and policies, essentially consistent with the recommendations of both the (World) Bank and the International Monetary Fund, have been steadfastly pursued since September 1973'.

Alliance for Profit

In 1976, Chile's Chicago Boys changed their strategy for meeting the country's external financing needs.

The debate about the junta's gross abuses of human rights had spread throughout the multilateral and bilateral agencies of the industrialised countries. Some northern nations had already cut off official development assistance for human rights reasons. The regime was dismayed and alarmed when the Carter Administration in the US, provoked by the assassination in Washington of a former Chilean ambassador, also began to apply human rights restrictions against Chile.

Instead of relying on official aid flows, including debt rescheduling and IMF credits, the authorities began to court private capital markets. The goal was to preserve the dictatorship's autonomy from external protests against its continuing human rights violations.

As a result, since 1976, net *official* financial flows to Chile have been negative. For the same reasons, Chile decided not to ask for another rescheduling of its debt payments in the Paris Club, where it expected further resistance. Nor was the IMF approached for another stand-by agreement. Not only did the regime want to avoid a contentious debate at the Fund, but the projected balance of payments deficit for 1976 was not so large as to require a new seal of approval, especially since the private banks were willing to fill the breach.

Chile was able to turn to the banks because of changing conditions in international capital markets. In the wake of the 1974-75 recession, and thanks to the flood of petro-dollars recycled from OPEC through international banks, private bankers found themselves with surplus capital in search of credit-worthy borrowers. But there were only so many prime borrowers to be found and the banks began to lend to countries which only recently had been unacceptable risks. In Chile's case, the credit-rating criteria that mattered to bankers, particularly financial indicators relating to the balance of payments and foreign exchange reserves, were improving by 1976. Perhaps more important, the military government had proven to international financiers its commitment to make any sacrifices (or rather to demand any sacrifices from its population) to repay its foreign debt. Pinochet's political grip now seemed more secure (at least in the medium term, the operative horizon for bankers) and bankers reasoned that a government dedicated to a free market and an open economy and not subject to scrutiny and opposition from domestic political sources, would be likely to be able to pay back its debts, even if times were difficult. Such a risk assessment was, of course, a political as much as a financial judgment.

⌐ In May 1976, Chile obtained its first important medium-term loan
on the private capital market. The loan was originally contingent upon
the junta entering a new agreement with the IMF. But when no
agreement was forthcoming, the banks agreed to go through with the
loan anyway, deeming the seal of approval unnecessary. From this
point of view, the sources of Chile's external finance shifted radically
from public to private entities. In 1975, two-thirds of Chile's total
foreign indebtedness stemmed from credits from multilateral
institutions and official organisations. By 1978, these same sources
provided only 8.8 per cent of the new net foreign debt incurred and by
1980, two-thirds of the total foreign debt of US$11.2 billion came
from private banks.

Dependence on private instead of official sources meant that Chile
had to borrow money at higher interest rates and to repay it within
shorter periods. This made foreign borrowing more costly to the
regime when international interest rates started to rise. But the
economic management team was willing to pay the price. Private bank
capital effectively allowed the junta to escape embarrassing debate on
its human rights record in international forums. The inflows of
private capital, more than US$5 billion from 1976 to 1980, also
reinforced the authority of the Chicago boys within government and
helped them impose their *laissez-faire* model.

⌐ The economic team claimed that these inflows of private funds
confirmed the wisdom of their policies (although, in this period,
communist regimes such as those of Poland and China also obtained
considerable loans from the Euro-dollar market). The Minister of
Finance went so far as to boast, in 1978, that 'our excellent image in
the world financial markets allows us access to foreign credit'. In fact,
the reverse was true: the junta's propaganda made use of private bank
support for Chile in order to improve the regime's tarnished image
abroad. In this way, the alliance between the banks and the junta
granted a mantle of respectability to an internationally isolated
dictatorship.

Miracle or Mirage?

From 1977 to mid-1981, Chile's economy registered impressive results
in expanding the Gross Domestic Product, reducing inflation and
diversifying exports. International business publications lauded the
achievements, monetarists claimed them as fruits of their theories,
and the Pinochet junta seized upon them as evidence of an 'economic
miracle'. The Chilean authorities also used selective data on the
country's economic performance to counter international

condemnations of the junta's human rights abuses. If political and civil liberties were not abundantly enjoyed in Chile, at least Chileans were thankful for the government's restoration of economic stability and growth. It was an argument that impressed some international observers. *Time* magazine noted in January 1981: 'For many economists who deplore its authoritarian government, Chile remains a model of what can be achieved in restructuring an ageing, prostrate economy into a streamlined machine'. Miracle status, in other words, became one of the junta's foremost arguments for legitimacy.

By the end of 1981, however, the 'miracle' was over and the Chilean economy plunged into recession. The government blamed the downturn on global economic conditions and claimed the 'open market' model was still viable. But the weaknesses in the so-called miracle could be assessed even before the onslaught of the recession.

Fundamental flaws had appeared in the model at the zenith of its application. The recession hit Chile especially hard because of these flaws. An examination of major social and economic indicators, beyond the superficial data advertised by the junta or the narrow range of indicators of importance to private banks, reveals that Chile's economic model was more mirage than miracle.

The expansion of economic output during the late 1970s must be put in perspective. The 7.7 per cent average annual growth of the GDP from 1977 to 1980 was in great part a recovery from the shock treatment of 1975. If the 1974-1980 period as a whole is considered, Chile's economic growth was much less than the Latin American average. On a *per capita* basis, the output of goods and services only returned to its 1972 level by the end of 1979.

But this recovery of production was accompanied by a regressive redistribution of wealth and by a faulty restructuring of the economy. Both processes were reinforced by the inflow of large amounts of foreign capital.

One of the main features of the economic model after 1973 was the growing concentration of wealth. Government decrees favoured the rapid expansion of financial enterprises by granting them freer access to foreign capital. Virtually every important economic grouping in Chile owned one or more large financial corporation which the new elite used to expand control over a large part of the country's industrial, mining and agricultural assets. Bankrupt firms and what used to be nationalised enterprises, since sold off by the junta at bargain prices, were brought up by these financial groups, often with the use of foreign loans. One study of post-coup corporate concentration shows how, by 1978, the top six economic clans controlled two-thirds of the total assets of Chile's largest 200 enterprises.

61

This concentration of wealth contributed to increasing economic inequality. By 1978, the richest fifth of the population enjoyed more than half of total national consumption, while the poorest 60 per cent of the people shared only 28 per cent. The fortunes of the rich were won directly at the expense of the bottom 60 per cent of income-earners.

In addition, the junta's decrees on wage controls, reduction in government employment and cuts in government spending, reinforced the unequal income distribution and even deepened impoverishment. By 1980, real wages and salaries were still inferior to their 1969 level

Distribution of Consumption by fifths of the Population

1969   **1978**

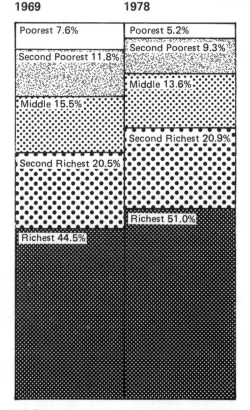

Source: INE, 'Encuestas de Presupuestos familiares', (1969 and 1978); *El Mercurio,* February 25, 1979.

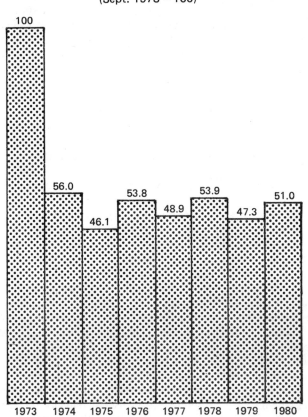

Index of Minimum Family Incomes, 1973-80
(Sept. 1973 = 100)

100

56.0   53.8   53.9   51.0
46.1   48.9   47.3

1973   1974   1975   1976   1977   1978   1979   1980

Source: ODEPLAN, Jose Aldunate and Jaime Ruiz-Tagle, 'La Casera y su economia de mercado', *Mensaje,* No. 294, November 1980.

and almost a third below their 1971 high. The poorest were especially hard-hit. Since 1973, the real value of the minimum family income earned by a fifth of the population had been cut in half. The 'social wages' of Chileans have also been squeezed. By 1979, both government expenditure as a whole and outlays for social programmes in particular, were 10 per cent less in real terms than in 1969. Spending on education, housing and health services remained well beneath the historical highs recorded under the previous government and as a result, serious social problems in these areas remain unsolved.

Unemployment has remained at unprecedented levels since the military coup and official statistics consistently underestimate unemployment by at least 5 per cent due to the exclusion of almost 200,000 persons engaged in a minimum employment programme at less than subsistence wages. While the national unemployment rate declined to 11 per cent in March 1981, it soared again a year later to 20 per cent.

A restructuring of the economy has indeed been achieved, much of it with the aid of external finance. Growth in the tertiary or service sector (up from 52.5 per cent of the economy in 1970 to 58 per cent in 1980) has been registered at the expense of the mining, agricultural and industrial sectors of the economy. Goods production as a whole declined from 1973 to 1979 while finance and banking activity, again, sectors enjoying access to foreign credit were the main contributors to economic expansion. The manufacturing sector suffered most. Many manufacturers never recovered from the shock treatment. A large number cut output and simply became importers. By 1980, industrial employment was 10 per cent less than in 1970 and 20 per cent below its 1973 level. Some diversification of exports was achieved, dependence on mineral exports declined from 83 per cent of the total exports by value in 1974 to 60 per cent in 1980. But the nation's export earnings remained highly dependent on natural resources and semi-processed materials, leaving Chile still very vulnerable to fluctuations in price and demand on international markets. Apart from the growth of the service sector, Chile has virtually become a 'hewer of wood and drawer of water.'

But the Achilles heel of the Chilean model is its failure to generate a sufficient amount of capital investment. If a country does not invest enough each year to replace worn-out or obsolete production facilities, the nation's productive capacity will deteriorate. If it fails to invest today in its production base, it will not have the ability to create new wealth tomorrow. Chile's capital investment levels, a traditional weakness in the economy, were about half of the Latin American average for the 1974-79 period and the recession dealt them a further setback.

This low level of capital investment points to a failure of the free market's 'invisible hand'. Part of the problem is due to the junta's intentional shrinking of the state's role in public works investment. It is also due to decisions by Chilean investors to put their savings into non-productive investments, including speculation, banking and corporate concentration. It is also because of the pattern of direct foreign investment; although the junta bent over backwards to attract direct foreign investment, actual inflows have not lived up to expectations and most of the investment that has materialised has involved use of existing enterprises or supported commercial activities instead of contributing to new capital investment.

Above all, the capital investment contradiction in the model is a reflection of how large inflows of borrowed capital have been squandered by Chile's new elite. Rich Chileans used foreign loans to go on an international buying spree. Imports of non-essential consumer goods (including furs, alcohol, carpets and home entertainment equipment) more than doubled from 1970 to 1978 in real terms and increased their share of total imports from 14 to 21 per cent. But, during the same period, capital goods imports remained static in nominal terms. The model's propensity towards imported consumption at the expense of capital investment and capital goods imports worsened in the 1979 to mid-1982 period, when the authorities maintained a fixed exchange rate and, in so doing, caused further damage to an already battered manufacturing sector. As the international investment review *Business Latin America* noted, with capital goods imports less than half of the value of non-essential imports, 'the purchasing binge will not translate into a powerful productive base in the next few years.'

The Chilean economy was on a dangerous debt treadmill. Pinochet's economic planners had hoped the opening of the economy would bring in foreign capital for investment. Instead, foreign borrowing has been mandatory simply to cover a growing current account deficit resulting from imported consumption and more borrowing has been needed to pay back the resultant short-term debts. In the 1975-79 period, the economy had to cover a US$2.9 billion current account deficit and at the same time find US$5.1 billion in foreign currency to pay off old external debts. By the end of 1981, Chile's gross external debt stood at US$15 billion, making it the second most indebted country (after Panama) *per capita* in the entire Third World

Since 1976, Chile's debt-service ratio has fluctuated between 40-50 per cent of its annual export earnings. The IMF usually considers a Third World country to be encountering a debt crisis when its debt-service ratio is consistently more than 20 per cent. In 1981, an unprecedented 58.4 per cent of foreign exchange earned by Chile's exports had to be allocated to service the foreign debt. But, with a low level of capital investment, the country was not generating the productive capacity to pay off its debt in the future.

Chile's situation was comparable to that of a deeply indebted and short-sighted businessman who was already burning up half of his income to pay past debts. He did so by gross and sometimes brutal exploitation of his labour force. But, because he continued to spend more money than he earned, this entrepreneur had to seek new loans

CHILE'S FOREIGN DEBT, 1970-81
(millions of US$)

	Gross Foreign Debt	Net Foreign Debt (less reserves)	Debt Service Ratio[a] (per cent)
1970	3,123	2,618	33%
1971	3,196	2,906	NA
1972	3,602	3,331	NA
1973	4,048	3,657	12%
1974	4,774	4,239	18%
1975	5,263	4,836	39%
1976	5,195	4,379	45%
1977	5,435	4,563	50%
1978	6,911	5,314	46%
1979	8,463	5,671	49%
1980	11,239	6,537	50%[e]
1981[e]	15,000		

a. net interest payments plus amortisation as percentage of exports of goods and services.
e. estimate.

Sources: Central Bank; CEPAL; Juan Guillermo Espinoza, 'Endeudamiento external: Cuanto, como y a que costó", *Análisis,* September-October 1980.

from the bank each year to maintain his bloated life-style and keep other creditors happy. Besides, because he invested little of his income or new loans in improving his business or upgrading his equipment, his future capacity to produce was deteriorating. He would soon face the prospect of bankruptcy.

IMF Policy versus Integral Development

Chile's experience shows that dependence on external finance is a key factor influencing government policies. Part of this dependence derives from the underdeveloped status of the Chilean economy, in particular, its character as a producer of minerals vulnerable to the fluctuations in international markets. The ideology of Chile's rulers has also determined the country's degree of independence. Despite external campaigns against it, the socialist and nationalist coalition formed by Allende resisted foreign financial pressures. In contrast, the military government which ousted Allende soon purged and repressed nationalist and progressive forces and made Chile open and vulnerable to the influence of international financial institutions. The price paid by Allende for striving for independence was extremely high, but not uncommon in the Third World. As a government dedicated to socialism and electoral democracy, the Popular Unity coalition had great difficulty in managing an economy in transition while trying to sustain both domestic political support (by providing material gains for its supporters) and access to international credit in a hostile international environment.

Under the military government, the monetarist philosophy of the IMF became official doctrine. At times the near-religious commitment of the junta to ultra-orthodoxy even surpassed the fervour of the Fund. But, throughout the 1974-1981 period, the model's relationship to, and dependence on, the IMF and private sources of capital was central to its existence. The IMF was able to exert direct and determinant influence on economic policy in 1975, the year shock treatment was applied and the model took on its complete shape. IMF seals of approval subsequently allowed the regime to wean the economy from official sources of external finance towards a heightened reliance on private bank sources. This change of sources allowed the junta to avoid external pressures because of its human rights record. After 1975, the continuing IMF approval of the Chicago Boys model plus the blessing of international banks, strengthened the position of the economic managers in the government. In this way, continuing international financial support for the junta sustained the regime's economic model. And, because the model required repression, the conclusion can be drawn that external finance has been instrumental in consolidating and perpetuating the gross violation of human rights in Chile.

The results of the Chilean model show how free market monetarism represents the antithesis of integral development. Instead of enhancing national sovereignty and self-reliance, the model made Chile more and more dependent on and subject to outside forces and influences. Instead of promoting social justice, the model widened inequalities and the divisions between social classes. Instead of increasing economic, social and political participation in society, the model reduced it, concentrating economic and political power in small wealthy groups, while the poor were excluded from economic as well as political decision-making.

Collapse of a Development Model

Today, Chile's showcase is in tatters. In February 1983, the government announced that it would stop repaying the principal on its

US$17 billion foreign debt while it worked out a rescheduling agreement with its foreign bank creditors. This move followed a US$900 million agreement with the IMF in anticipation of rescheduling US$3.5 billion of the foreign debt. A further US$1 billion of new loans was also being sought.

This financial impasse followed a year in which the Chilean economy recorded a massive 13 per cent fall in output, by far the worst result for any Latin American country. Unemployment reached 25.2 per cent in Santiago in 1983, although that figure does not include the thousands of people employed on meagre wages by the Government's emergency work programme. A total of 431 bankruptcies was recorded during 1982 and, by the end of the year, Chile had accumulated a US$4.8 billion trade deficit.

Although the world recession has compounded Chile's problems, low commodity prices (copper, Chile's main export, fetched the same price in mid-1983 in real terms as it had 15 years previously) and high interest rates are not solely to blame. The government's insistence on maintaining an overvalued currency made foreign borrowing relatively attractive, but also led to dramatic falls in reserves and hindered the country's exporters, whose products were overpriced on international markets. By mid-1982, the ever-worsening trade deficit forced the government to devalue the peso. Dollar debtors were hard-hit as they now had to come up with more pesos in order to meet their dollar obligations.

The devaluation forced many producers into bankruptcy because they were unable to service their large foreign loans. These bankruptcies created a severe liquidity crisis in the country's banking system. In January 1983, the government stepped in to take over five banks. This move, which included the country's two biggest banks, the Banco de Chile and the Banco de Santiago, was 'made necessary by the magnitude of the anticipated loan portfolio losses', according to the government. The banking sector, which had benefited from the overvalued peso during the previous two years, was badly hit by their customers' inability to repay their debts at the devalued exchange rate. To forestall a total collapse of the national banking system, the government was forced to undertake a massive intervention which ran totally against its free-market philosophy.

Furthermore, Chile's foreign creditors were anxious that the government should take over responsibility for the country's private sector foreign debt (about 64 per cent of the total). This had long been resisted as the government argued that taking over such a debt would violate sacred economic principles. However, those foreign creditors with loans outstanding to Chilean companies feared their loans would not be repaid if the government did not help. Using Chile's need to renegotiate its debt as a lever, these foreign creditors forced the government to take responsibility for more than half of the private sector debt, in the wake of a series of 12 bankrupticies of companies belonging to the country's two largest conglomerates. This again represented a big break with the past.

In March 1983, the government began to lend to other companies which had fallen behind on their debt service. A total of US$15 million was loaned to eight companies to enable them to avoid liquidation. The government's decision to intervene in the economy was a dramatic departure from its monetarist policies. The failure of orthodox, free-market policies to provide a stable basis for growth, much less a basis for equitable development, has devastated the doctrines of the Chicago Boys. Paradoxically, the model has been breached at the behest of international private sector creditors, whose interests are supposedly served by such a model.

It is the Chilean people who bore the social and political cost of the Chicago experiment; the Pinochet regime will also expect them to bear the cost of its collapse. But, by 1983, it was clear that this was unacceptable to the majority of Chileans. Throughout the year, opposition grew rapidly into a mass movement aimed at the removal of the Pinochet dictatorship. It soon became apparent that Pinochet was destined to fall, following the collapse of the economic policies he had done so much to sustain.

5 Peru: The Bankers go it alone

In 1968 a military coup with a difference took place in Peru. In Latin America the military normally intervenes to defend the ruling oligarchy, but the Peruvian armed forces stepped in to overthrow such an oligarchy. So as to understand the reasons for this, we must briefly look at the structure of the Peruvian economy and society at the same time.

Peru is a country five times larger than Britain, with a population of 18 million people. It is divided into the desert Pacific coast (with 43 per cent of the population), the barren mountains of the Andes (47 per cent of the population) and the Amazonian rain forest (10 per cent of the population). The country shows the classic features of a developing country that produces primary commodities. For centuries, it has been integrated into the world economy through the changing foreign demand for a series of primary products. This export demand, rather than internal demand based on the needs of the bulk of the population, has constituted the main engine for economic growth. As a result Peru's economic fate has always been highly dependent on forces beyond its control. Whenever overseas demand has slumped or a natural resource has become exhausted, growth has slowed down until accelerated by a revival of foreign demand. Peruvian economic history has been one of cyclical periods of booms and slumps.

This extreme dependence on exports has given rise to a dual economy in which a high-productivity, capital-intensive and export-oriented modern sector generates about 60 per cent of total production yet employs less than a quarter of the labour force. The bulk of the labour force is absorbed by a low-productivity, subsistence-oriented traditional sector. This dual structure of the economy also determines the low income of the majority of the population in the traditional sector and the concentration of earnings in the modern sector. So, by the 1960s, Peru had one of the least equal distributions of income in the world, with the poorest 20 per cent of the population receiving only 3.5 per cent of personal income. Because investment took place overwhelmingly in the modern, export sector, there arose a chronic local food supply problem as crop production stagnated through lack of investment. This stagnation stimulated rapid migration from rural to urban areas in response to the demand for petty services generated by the modern sector. At the same time, the industrial sector remained relatively underdeveloped, based on a very small market.

By the late 1960s, the country's economy was running out of steam. Although it exhibited a very diversified export structure by comparison with many developed countries (copper, zinc, iron, lead, silver, fishmeal, sugar, cotton and wool together comprised 95 per cent of total exports), the growth rate of exports slowed through the 1960s. This in turn led to a decline in the rate of investment and a growing balance of payments deficit, and thus to a reduction in the overall rate of economic growth. The main reason for the slowdown in exports was the fall in raw material production resulting from poor prospects for export demand. Local exporters were reluctant to re-invest profits to bring new production on stream (for example, in irrigation schemes to increase agricultural production) and increasing output in the important fishmeal industry was hampered by ecological factors. Furthermore, during the 1960s, mining exports came increasingly under the control of foreign companies which were unwilling to invest in new mining ventures, given the poor demand forecasts.

All this led to growing dissatisfaction with both the role of the landed oligarchy and with that of foreign companies. Both were seen as exercising a stranglehold over the development potential of the economy. In the case of agriculture, according to the 1961 census, three-quarters of the land were under the control of less than 1 per cent of the land-owners. Foreign capital, on the other hand, controlled more than half of total exports by 1968, including three-quarters of mining exports, two-thirds of sugar exports and half of fishing, cotton and wool processing. While some critics advocated reforms in order simply to regenerate the growth of exports, more radical critics called for structural reforms in order to overcome the basic dualism of the economy by re-orienting it away from its dependence on exports. This was seen as the only way to bring about rapid improvement in the living standards of the bulk of the population in the traditional sector.

The Velasco Government

The military reformers, led by General Velasco, who came to power in 1968, proposed a radical restructuring of Peruvian society by a 'third way', which was neither capitalist nor communist. Their stated aim was to create a society which would be 'pluralist, humanistic and based on social democracy with full participation'. They attributed the sluggishness of exports and the general lack of dynamism in the economy during the 1960s to the excessive power and influence of foreign companies and their allies in the landed oligarchy. They attempted to remedy this by asserting greater state control over the profits earned by exporters and by opening opportunities for local industrialists. New tax laws were passed to encourage the import of machinery in order to promote industrialisation and subsidies were offered for the export of non-traditional manufactured goods. Industrialists also benefited from price subsidies designed to keep down the cost of food and public transport to workers. The key role of the state was to build up a heavy industrial sector, making the economy more self-reliant and less vulnerable to the vagaries of international demand for its exports of products.

Despite the vague rhetoric of the new regime, decisions were taken which gained it a measure of support from the political left in the country. Six days after the coup, the government nationalised the International Petroleum Company (IPC), a subsidiary of the Rockefeller family's corporate empire, based in the US. The refusal to meet the demands by the parent company for compensation soon gave the regime an international image as anti-imperialist. Expropriation of IPC was followed by the creation of a giant new state oil company, Petroperú, which immediately began exploration in the Amazon region. In 1969, the military launched an agrarian reform programme under which the large private sugar estates of the northern coast were taken over. By 1975, almost all of the landed oligarchy had been expropriated and their large holdings turned into state co-operatives, nominally under peasant control. The reform affected nearly half of the arable land and, by 1975, about five million hectares of land had been re-allocated to nearly 200,000 families.

In 1970, US mining companies were deprived of their undeveloped concessions and a new state company, Mineroperú, was given the monopoly of mineral export marketing and development of new mining projects. By the mid-1970s, the state had assumed the role previously held by foreign capital in mining and petroleum. The state had taken over an important part of the banking sector, virtually all export marketing, the entire fishing sector, the railways and the country's international airlines. According to one calculation, the share of foreign capital in the economy was reduced from 21 to 8 per cent of GNP during the period 1968-75, while the share of the state rose to 26 per cent.

The traditional landed oligarchy was the most hard hit by the reforms. On the other hand, the military also suppressed strikes, closed leftist publications and deported trade union and leftist leaders. The regime, however, was not opposed to foreign investment in principle. While nationalisations took place in industries involved in the exploration of basic natural resources, such as mining, foreign capital was encouraged in new joint ventures where prospects of long-term profit were high. At the same time, because the state was rapidly becoming the principle investor, it was more interested in foreign loans than direct foreign investment.

The reform programme required a massive increase in public investment. Since the military was not prepared to squeeze the rich to pay for it through reforms in the income tax system, it turned to foreign borrowing as an easy way out. A number of grandiose development projects were started with large imported components — an oil pipeline across the Andes, extensive irrigation projects and several new fishing ports.

The growth of the public sector was reflected in the construction of the new ministerial and state corporation buildings needed to house the expanding public sector bureaucracy.

Because of the nationalisation of IPC and the anti-imperialist rhetoric of the regime, the US government cut off all aid loans to Peru after 1968 and reduced World Bank and Inter-American Bank loans to a trickle by using its voting power in those institutions. However, the regime was able to overcome this official credit blockade by forging links with international private banks. Because of the stagnation in the traditional loan market in the developed countries, and because of the rapid growth in supply of deposits following the oil price increases in the early 1970s, bankers were showing an unaccustomed interest in lending to less-developed countries. As a result of this fortuitous coincidence of interest, in 1972 Peru was able to borrow US$147 million on the eurocurrency market, and US$734 million in 1973, making it the third largest borrower among developing countries in the latter year. These loans dramatically increased the Peruvian public sector foreign debt, which trebled in six years to total US$3 billion in 1974.

For a number of years, the economy appeared healthy, growing at an average rate of 5.5 per cent from 1969 to 1973. Industrial output grew at a rate of 7.1 per cent a year, the trade balance remained positive and the annual inflation rate was kept down to about 7 per cent. But this impressive performance masked the underlying vulnerability of growing dependence on external finance — a vulnerability which would soon come to the surface and precipitate an economic crisis. External financing of the massive public investment programme was defended in the belief that it would generate a rapid expansion of exports, which would be sufficient to repay the original debt. In this respect the military placed great store on what turned out to be over-optimistic forecasts of future oil and copper production. The heavily subsidised industrial sector was consuming massive amounts of foreign exchange, which had to be paid for by export of primary products or by foreign loans. At the same time, the trade unions fought for and won an improvement in real wages, which reached a peak in 1972. Meanwhile, domestic food supply was not keeping pace with demand, giving rise to inflationary pressure. The situation was made worse by a growing public sector deficit, as income tax revenue failed to keep pace with the boom in public spending.

The impending crisis was triggered off in 1974 by a sharp deterioration in the balance of trade which showed a deficit for the first time since 1968. While the value of exports increased by 35 per cent between 1973 and 1974, that of imports almost doubled. The fishmeal industry, a major foreign exchange earner, collapsed in 1973 as a result of over-fishing and exports only held up thanks to a short-lived boom in world commodity prices in the wake of the OPEC oil price increases in that year. The massive increase in imports was largely due to the rapid expansion of public investment, which rose by 56 per cent in 1974, in a wide range of mining, agro-industrial and petroleum projects.

The appearance of a trade deficit was made worse by the commencement of repayment obligations on previous foreign borrowing. The country's payments deficit in 1974 soared to US$725 million compared to only US$174 million the previous year. This deficit was financed in turn by more borrowing from the euromarket as well as by a resumption of official credits from the US, following the signing in February 1974 of an agreement with Washington under which the Peruvian government agreed to pay compensation of US$150 million for the assets of the 11 US companies expropriated since 1968. This compensation payment would itself be financed by a loan from the US banks, thereby deepening Peru's indebtedness.

In 1975, the economic crisis worsened as the country's balance of payments deteriorated and the budget deficit doubled. Workers struggled to maintain their real living standards against rising inflation. Shop-floor dissatisfaction with the main trade union body, the CGTP, grew as its moderate leaders continued to lend tacit support to the Velasco regime because of its progressive character. Emergency economic measures taken in June included a 20-30 per cent increase in the price of basic consumer goods as subsidies were reduced in a vain attempt to cut the budget deficit and the rate of inflation. The economic growth rate faltered as demand fell and unemployment rose.

By now it was apparent that in fact the reforms had only benefited a small part of the population. The agrarian reform had converted the large landholdings into state-controlled production units but the vast bulk of the poverty-stricken rural population, who survived as independent producers remained unaffected. Industrial workers had gained little from the marginal participation in the management and ownership of companies under the participatory schemes of the regime. Even domestic industrialists, who were being fostered by the regime, were divided in their loyalty. As a result, Velasco was unable to consolidate a strong political backing for his programme.

As the onset of the economic crisis revealed the inherent weaknesses of the Velasco model, the coalition which he had held together since 1968 disintegrated. Divisions appeared within the military, with rightists fearing the increasingly independent political mobilisation of workers and peasants in defence of their living standards. In August 1975 Velasco was ousted by General Francisco Morales Bermúdez, the Prime Minister. The military presented this new 'second phase' of the regime as a mere continuation of the 'first phase'. Yet the change was clearly to the right, as leftist military officers were forced to retire and more orthodox economic policies were introduced.

Going It Alone

Despite the coup within the coup, the economic crisis continued to worsen. The total value of exports fell in 1975 as the expected oil bonanza failed to materialise, the anchovy schools virtually disappeared from the fishing grounds and world copper prices tumbled. Nor could imports be drastically cut in line with the decline of exports, in order to reduce the trade deficit without bringing the economy to a standstill. On top of a massive trade deficit, expected to be US$740 million for the year, debt service obligations for 1976 were already US$500 million. The balance of payments crisis was so serious that new foreign borrowing was urgently required to avoid a default on outstanding debt obligations. In January 1976, another round of austerity measures was announced and in February, during a visit to Lima, Henry Kissinger, the US Secretary of State, told Morales Bermúdez that future US aid would depend on Peru showing a more friendly attitude to the US government and US private investors.

The normal way for Peru to proceed in such a balance of payments crisis would have been to borrow from the IMF. By signing a letter of intent with the Fund, Peru would have gained renewed access to credits from international agencies and private bankers. However, as the price for granting its seal of approval, the IMF would have demanded the implementation of a drastic stabilisation programme which the military leaders of the 'second phase' were loathe to implement, given their still shaky political foundation.

Instead, in March 1976, the government turned to the same US banks which, in the early 1960s, had been competing with each other in the rush to lend to Peru and requested a major balance of payments loan. In July, in an unprecedented move which attracted international attention, a consortium of six US banks, led by Citibank, agreed to a five-year loan of US$200 million without Peru having signed a prior agreement with the IMF. The banks behaved in this unusual manner because of their growing fear of an imminent Peruvian default. The outstanding foreign debt already stood at US$3 billion, one of the largest among developing countries, half of which was owed to private banks, including US$1.5 billion to US banks alone. A default on this scale would have set an extremely dangerous precedent, just when the banks were increasing their lending to developing countries. Bankers reasoned that Morales Bermúdez had to be supported at all costs against the mounting strength of the trade union movement and the political Left, which advocated a debt moratorium. After all, 1975 had been the most conflictive year so far in Peruvian labour history. Nearly a third of all the wage labourers in Peru had been involved in 779 strikes, which had cost industry 20.3 million working hours.

In order to lessen the risk inherent in further lending to Peru without the protective shield of the IMF, the banks imposed their own set of conditions in an attempt to ensure that Peru would generate sufficient foreign exchange to pay service obligations arising from past loans. The agreement between the banks and the Peruvian government covered the following areas:

i. reduction of state intervention in the economy and selling off some state companies, beginning with the anchovy fleet:
ii. increased efforts to assist the private sector;

iii. more favourable treatment of foreign investment, including the re-opening of Peru to exploration by foreign oil companies;
iv. an austerity programme including devaluation, price increases and spending cuts.

The most controversial aspect of the agreement, however, was the provision that the banks would monitor the performance of the government to make sure that it met the various economic targets. This was the first time since the 1920s that private banks had interfered so directly in the domestic affairs of a Latin American government. The loan was to be disbursed in two halves. The first would be released immediately but the second would be dependent on the banks agreeing, after a few months, that the government had kept to its economic targets.

The Peruvian government may have believed that it was lessening the ties of financial dependency by borrowing directly from the private banks and avoiding the IMF, but in fact its future room for maneouvre was being even further circumscribed. For the banks which had organised the loan cleverly ensured that the risk was spread very widely among the international banking community. The six US banks placed half of their own share with smaller US banks and they made the US$200 million loan itself conditional on a further US$200 million being raised from private banks in Europe, Canada and Japan. In this way, the opportunity for Peru to play off one part of the banking community against another in the future would be minimised. Given such a wide involvement in Peruvian foreign debt, the doors of the international banking community would be completely shut to Peru if it ever tried to effect a partial default.

As a result of the contradictions of the development strategy pursued by the military, the rate of economic growth slowed down from an average of 6.3 per cent in 1972-74 to 3.5 in 1975 and 2.8 in 1976. The slump in output was heaviest in industry and construction; the biggest losers were wage and salary earners. On 28 June 1976 the government announced its most drastic austerity package yet as part of the conditions agreed with the private banks. It included a large devaluation, cuts in government spending, a freeze on the hiring of staff and cuts in subsidies to state enterprises. Food prices were allowed to rise by another 25-30 per cent and the purchasing power of wages fell back to the 1968 level. The gains to workers' living standards won during the first phase had been completely wiped out. Spontaneous protests mushroomed throughout the shanty-towns which surrounded Lima. The government retaliated by imposing a night curfew and closing down leftist newspapers. In July, three leading military leftists in the cabinet were dismissed and, on August

13 the right to strike was abolished and the dismissal of workers who violated the 'national emergency' was permitted. These measures, which were renewed every month, greatly reduced the level of strike activity.

The unfavourable image of 'Wall Street Imperialism', which the banks were creating for themselves through their direct involvement in Peruvian economic management, led to their growing reluctance to risk further political involvement, especially as it became clear by the end of the year that they had still been unable to solve Peru's economic crisis. Morgan Guaranty was the most vocal bank in arguing that they should retire to their traditional seats in the wings and let the IMF get on with the job of doing the dirty work for them. The unsatisfactory experience of 'going it alone' in Peru did more than anything else to persuade the banks of the pivotal role of the IMF as the institution best suited to impose on debtor countries in the Third World those harsh economic conditions needed to ensure the profitability of the international banks.

Returning to the Fold

By the beginning of 1977, the situation had still not improved. The banks refused then to release the second half of their loan unless the government were to come to an agreement with the IMF. The banks knew that the Fund would demand more stringent conditions than they had been able to impose the previous year, when they had been fearful of forcing the government to the wall. The success of the government in quelling the protest provoked by the austerity measures of the previous June suggested that the political climate was not as explosive as they had believed. These measures reflected a definitive shift in the balance of political power and the banks became confident that, in any showdown, the right would come out on top.

The Peruvian government agreed, therefore, to receive a mission from the IMF, which arrived in March 1977. In classic IMF fashion, it diagnosed Peru's illness as a misallocation of resources caused by excessive state intervention. The treatment proposed was drastic — the country's balance of payments crisis was to be corrected without further international loans and inflation was to be kept to a maximum of 15 per cent during 1977. In order to achieve these objectives, the mission proposed: harsh spending cuts in all public enterprises, leaving them to balance their books by price rises; an increase in petroleum prices to eliminate the deficit of Petroperú and to provide a surplus for central government; a sharp cut in the purchase of machinery, mostly imported, for public sector investment projects;

elimination of all import quotas, a 30 per cent devaluation of the currency and, finally, wage rises were to be restricted to 10 per cent a year.

The programme was a recipe for zero growth, the political implications of which were intolerable, even to officials of Peru's conservative central bank, who threatened to resign if the programme was accepted. They proposed an alternative set of more flexible proposals which would not have had such a traumatic effect on the economy, while the minister of industry put forward a plan to expand the economy.

Months of political indecision followed. Luis Barlúa, the finance minister, resigned and was succeeded by Walter Piazza, the first private sector businessman appointed to a cabinet post since 1968. Piazza negotiated a modified agreement with the Fund, involving a higher budget deficit and inflation rate, but this was rejected by the cabinet and he too resigned.

Nevertheless, substantial price rises were implemented, arousing strong popular protest which culminated in the first general strike in Peru since 1919. As dawn broke on 19 June 1977, workers in the squatters' settlements which surround Lima had already blockaded highways that lead to the city centre, threatening to burn any bus which tried to pass. Despite the strike's success in the capital, the communist-dominated CGTP labour confederation decided unexpectedly to call off the planned second day of the stoppage. The hard-won unity was broken, leaving workers confused and exposed to government repression. The police and army dispersed protestors the following day, killing 10 workers. Hundreds were arrested and laws suspended so as to allow factory owners to sack strikers. Because of that, 6,000 workers lost their jobs in the succeeding weeks, a blow which momentarily weakened the trade union movement.

By now the revolutionary and nationalist rhetoric of the military regime had a hollow ring to it. Corporate schemes for worker participation were in disarray, while the prestige of the military, whose economic policies had contributed to the radicalisation of the labour movement, had reached an all-time low. Its non-aligned and anti-imperialist stance had been replaced by subservience to the IMF. So few were surprised when, in November 1977, Morales Bermúdez announced plans for a gradual return to civilian rule, starting with elections to a Constituent Assembly in June 1978. Sensing the lull in trade union militancy, the government signed a stand-by agreement with the IMF which differed little from the Piazza proposals the cabinet had rejected. Peru would receive a US$100 million loan, released in bi-monthly instalments over two years. The IMF exacted harsh conditions. The 1978 budget deficit was to be cut to a third of that of the previous year and the corresponding rate of inflation by a half.

The first instalment was handed over in December, but, in February 1978, a Fund mission returned to Lima and declared Peru in gross violation of the agreed targets. The IMF refused further disbursements under the loan. This was a signal for the private banks to call off a proposed US$260 million loan, then under negotiation, and for the US government also to refuse further assistance.

The failure of the stand-by agreement placed Peru in an even tighter strait-jacket than before, since the withdrawal of the IMF's seal of approval cut it off from the international finance required to service its foreign debt. Peru was scheduled to pay debt service obligations in 1978 of US$1 billion on an outstanding debt of about US$8 billion of which US$4.8 billion was owed by the public sector. The debt service burden was so high then that, for every dollar coming into the country from export earnings, 55 cents were already committed to payments of interest and principal on foreign debt. There were no foreign reserves left in the central bank, the IMF having effectively cut off all foreign credit lines at a stroke. As one commentator put it at the time, 'the government of Morales Bermúdez is now squeezed from all sides. On the one hand, without IMF support the country cannot obtain the credit needed to meet its existing debt obligations and pay for expensive food imports. On the other hand, the steps demanded by the IMF have led to the riots, general strikes and upheavals that jeopardise the nation's planned return to civilian democratic government'.

Without quick action, imports would have to be cut drastically, throwing thousands out of work and cutting food supplies. The banks and the IMF tightened the screws, insisting on further austerity measures as a condition for extending emergency relief. The government had survived the riots and strikes of 1977 and, by May 1978, felt itself strong enough to push through a further series of austerity measures which could lay the foundation for a new agreement with the IMF. So, on May 15, the most draconian austerity package yet was announced. Overnight, the cost of fuel, public transport and such basic foodstuffs as milk and cooking oil were doubled as government subsidies were ended in an attempt to reduce the budget deficit. Coming during already galloping inflation, the measures quickly provoked street clashes in Lima and strikes throughout provincial cities. After more than a dozen people had been killed, martial law was imposed and hundreds of leftist leaders were arrested and deported to Argentina. Popular sympathy swung decisively behind the more class-conscious and militant unions, which forced the CGTP leadership to call a second two-day general strike for

May 22 and 23. The strike was far more effective than that of the previous year. Lima was brought to a complete standstill as shanty-town dwellers again blocked every main road to the city centre. Work stopped throughout the country, from the mining centres of the Andes to the fishing ports on the Pacific coast. At least 30 people were killed in various parts of Peru during clashes between police and demonstrators.

Within days of the new austerity measures and with the sound of strikes and rioting in the streets, the banks agreed to roll over about US$200 million in repayments owed them during 1978, although interest was still to be paid. The deal itself was subject to a new stand-by arrangement being agreed with the IMF (which in fact was signed in September) and involved further cuts in government spending and another devaluation. This agreement opened the door to the complete rescheduling of the official foreign debt through the Paris Club, when foreign governments agreed to postpone 90 per cent of the debt service payments owed them by Peru in 1979 and 1980. These were turned into seven-year loans with a three-year grace period. Similar arrangements were made with the private banks.

Despite the tense political situation, the Constituent Assembly elections took place as scheduled on 18 June 1978. They provided a dramatic indication of the growing strength of the Left, which had never been considered as an electoral force to be reckoned with. For despite internal divisions and despite having been forced underground a month before the poll took place, the Left won 30 per cent of the vote. Many of the leaders arrested in May were elected to the assembly and the government was forced to allow their release from jail or return from exile.

The dramatic increase in the organised political support for the Left was a direct consequence of the economic policies imposed by the IMF — policies which were denounced during the election camapign. The elections took place during what had been officially declared 'The Year of Austerity' (although workers called it 'The Year of Misery'). This was a formal recognition by the government that solving the economic crisis meant cutting someone's income. The question was — whose income? The IMF ostensibly washed its hands of the whole problem, blandly taking the view that it was up to the government to decide the appropriate burdens of adjustment for various sectors of society. Yet a class bias was built into the IMF conditions themselves. When the IMF called for prices to be 'freed' while wages should be 'frozen', those who sold only their labour power and owned no capital would suffer the consequences.

In a society like that of Peru, already characterised by great inequality and social injustice, it was evident that the poor would bear

81

the economic cost of meeting the crisis. In 1977, the GDP declined by
1.2 per cent and, in 1978, by a further 1.8 per cent. From 1975 to 1979,
wage earners in Lima lost up to half of their purchasing power. One
hard-nosed banker was forced to admit: 'In a country as poor as Peru,
an austerity package often means pushing people into the starvation
zones'. That this happened as a result of the implementation of IMF
policies has been graphically and extensively documented in numerous
scientific surveys, which have shown how the fall in the purchasing
power of incomes and increases in unemployment had resulted in a
reduction in calorie intake, a rise in infant morality and a growth in
the reported cases of tuberculosis. Yet no amount of statistics can
hope to transmit the enormous personal suffering imposed on a
people who were already living on the breadline. Researchers in two
Lima squatter settlements revealed that 88 per cent of those who had
drunk milk regularly in 1972 no longer did so by 1978. Evaporated
milk, once the mainstay for weaning small children, had become a
luxury and instead mothers resorted to weak tea. By 1979, Nicovita, a
chicken feed containing a number of toxic substances but costing less
than 9p a kilo, was being eaten by squatter dwellers and peasants
alike. Most dramatic of all was the growth of under-employment,
which rose to include 50 per cent of the economically active
population. The number of street hawkers swelled in the city centre,
jamming the pavements as the wives and children of unemployed
factory workers sought desperately to make ends meet. On the main
highways in the city, the number of small children selling magazines
and sweets, and cleaning car windscreens in the few seconds before the
traffic lights changed, rose alarmingly. Petty crime escalated and a
flourishing second-hand market developed in car lights and
windscreen wipers stolen from parked cars. Such activities could do
little, however, to ease the overwhelming burden that IMF austerity
measures imposed on the already poor majority of Peruvians.

History repeats itself

Following its impressive result in the Constituent Assembly elections,
the United Left collapsed in the run-up to the presidential elections of
1980, which marked the full return to civilian rule. Five different left-
wing candidates competed and their combined vote totalled only 16
per cent. The election was won by the leader of the centre-right *Acción
Popular* (Popular Action) party, Fernando Belaúnde Terry, who had
been overthrown as president by the military reformers in 1968.

As a result of the harsh deflationary policies imposed by the IMF in
the wake of the crisis of 1977-78, the unemployment rate by then

stood at 10 per cent, and under-employment at 50 per cent, of the labour force. Nevertheless, the foreign trade situation had improved markedly by the time Belaúnde re-assumed the presidency. The balance of trade had gone into surplus after four years of deficit. Exports had expanded, thanks to a surge in world copper and silver prices, the completion of the trans-Andean oil pipeline and new mining output coming on stream. Meanwhile, growth in imports was still held down by the effects of the economic recession. For the time being, the foreign debt could be ignored, although it had climbed to US$9 billion, of which US$1 billion was short-term.

Encouraged by the favourable foreign trade situation and following clearly in the footsteps of his military predecessors, Belaúnde launched an ambitious plan for massive expansion of production of primary commodities for export during 1981-85, which would reinforce the dualist model of the Peruvian economy. In May 1981, Manuel Ulloa, the Prime Minister, led a mission to Paris to seek finance for no fewer than 88 investment projects with a total cost of US$11.5 billion, of which US$4.7 billion was required in foreign finance. Economically, the sale of public corporations to the private sector continued. Measures were enacted to attract foreign private investment and reduce the level of protection for domestic industry against competing imports.

But, by the end of 1981, Peru's balance of payments was under severe pressure. Export revenue had fallen due to the slump in raw material prices caused by the world recession. Rising interest rates meant that debt servicing was consuming 55 per cent of export revenue. Once again, the IMF was called in because of what the cabinet described as 'unmanageable external disequilibrium'. In a vain attempt to head off the barrage of criticism that an approach to the IMF (and acceptance of an austerity programme) would cause, central bank President, Richard Webb, argued, 'it is important that the stabilisation programme is seen as *ours* not *theirs!*'

The agreement signed in April 1982, and formally approved three months later, made a little more than US$1 billion available to Peru from the Extended Fund and Compensatory Financing Facilities. Yet the austerity measures that accompanied this agreement failed to compensate for the essential contradiction which the open-market economic policies of the Belaúnde government imposed on the economy. This contradiction is illustrated by the fortunes of two important export industries — mining and textiles. The falling world prices of metals (over which Peru has no control) cost the country US$400 million in lost export revenue in 1982. The national mining companies therefore demanded an extra US$200 million in extra credit so as to survive the recession. They also planned to lay off 33 per cent of their workers. The emphasis on exports of raw materials thus forced the country into further foreign borrowing, while jobs were lost even so. The Belaúnde government had tried also to encourage exports of manufactured goods but even this was fraught with problems. In November 1982, the US imposed a 30 per cent tariff on imports of Peruvian textiles. This effectively closed the US market to Peruvian exports — a catastrophic blow for the textile industry in Peru.

In the first five months of 1983, the Peruvian economy was contracting at an annual rate of 9 per cent. As local companies went bankrupt and repudiated their debts to local banks, a chain of bank collapses ensued. Ironically, it was left to the government to step in to mitigate the worst effects of such bankruptcies in the financial sector. This conflicted directly with the government's *laissez faire* policies.

By March 1983, Peru had joined the international debt queue as it attempted to re-finance US$2.2 billion in short-term foreign debts and to obtain US$400 million in new long-term loans. As for the new long-term loan, the cost was described as, 'an astronomical *Libor* plus 2.25 per cent'. 'It's a very reasonable package', commented one New York banker.

Although Peru has successfully re-financed its foreign debts, the present open-market economic policies offer little hope for improved employment opportunities or increased living standards for the majority of Peruvians. In fact, according to Merrill Lynch, a New York financial consultancy, Peru's attempts to attract foreign investment (the lynch-pin of the model) is hindered by precisely those pieces of legislation that defend the rights of Peruvian workers, notably the system of worker participation in management, as well as laws on job security and the activities of transnational corporations in Peru, especially with regard to sending profits abroad. As the Belaúnde government dismantles these safeguards, the plight of the poorest sections of the population will continue to deteriorate.

Only a different strategy could reverse this situation. It would have to overcome the basic dualism of the Peruvian economy by giving priority to the basic needs of the population, rather than to foreign demand for primary commodities, and by stressing domestic rather than external accumulation as the engine of growth. Such a strategy, however, would have to relegate the role of foreign trade to a secondary factor in the process of development, and would thus meet the determined opposition of the IMF, the international bankers and the transnational corporations.

6 The IMF and Democratic Socialism in Jamaica

The 1980 general election in Jamaica marked the end of the 'democratic socialist' government of Michael Manley. Following a bloody election campaign, his government was thrown out in a landslide defeat that was unprecedented in Jamaica's 38 years of adult suffrage. There is no doubt that the IMF, in conjunction with the international banks, played a major role in bringing down Manley's 'progressive' government.

However, it is insufficient to focus only on Manley as a victim of IMF intervention. Such analysis leads inevitably to a sense of hopelessness with regard to the prospects of radical regimes in the Third World. This chapter will therefore examine the contradictions of the Manley government itself, which paved the way for the devastation the IMF was to bring upon the Jamaican people.

The Era of Growth

During the 1950s and 1960s, the Jamaican economy experienced unprecedented growth. Annual growth rates averaged 6.7 per cent and real GDP more than doubled from 1959 to 1972. This growth was combined with high levels of capital investment (23.3 per cent of GDP in 1968). Although the balance of payments remained in deficit, this could be financed by inflows of foreign investment, mainly in the mining sector.

However, if one looks beyond the aggregate economic indicators, at the details of the economic edifice, major cracks can be found in the economy which would lead to the economic crisis of the 1970s.

One of the most important features of the Jamaican economy during the 1950s and 1960s was its remarkable dependence upon the bauxite and alumina industry. This sector grew at a faster rate than the growth of GDP itself. From 1950 to 1971, the mining sector grew at an annual rate of 16.3 per cent while GDP grew at only 10.4 per cent. Bauxite and alumina came to account for aproximately 75 per cent of Jamaica's export earnings. An examination of the relationship between the bauxite industry and economic growth in the economy as a whole shows that very high levels of foreign investment in the mining sector stimulated other areas of the economy. For example, 48 per cent of total capital investment from 1960 to 1971 was accounted for by the construction industry which supplied the bauxite industry with the processing plants, roads and other infrastructure needed. Such construction, in its turn, had a multiplier effect on the rest of the economy. Thus it created demand for local building materials and construction supply industries, and financed a high level of consumer demand through the wages paid to the construction workers.

In addition, the bauxite industry was a major supplier of the precious foreign exchange that the economy needed to meet its persistent balance of payments deficit in the current account (that is, the deficit in the export and import of goods and services). Of the net capital inflows to Jamaica from 1950 to 1956, 59 per cent was for investment in the bauxite industry. By 1964 US$650 million had been invested in that industry from abroad. The importance of this source of foreign exchange cannot be underestimated. It was used to finance the import of plant and machinery for other non-bauxite industries; it financed the import of raw materials and intermediate goods needed in local manufacturing, construction, transport, power generation and other services and, by encouraging foreign trade, it generated higher tax revenues for the government. In the longer run, the government hoped that, by investing this foreign exchange in the export sector, future foreign exchange earnings could be further increased.

However, this process made growth in a range of sectors totally dependent on continuing foreign investment in the bauxite industry. Once that investment slowed down or stopped, the effects would be felt throughout the economy. By the beginning of the 1970s, such a slow-down was occurring and growth in the bauxite industry fell to 30 per cent of its previous levels. This precipitated a deep crisis in the

Jamaican economy. Contrary, therefore, to the stable appearance of the Jamaican economy during the 1950s and 1960s, it was in fact perched precariously on the growth of one sector — and a sector which was totally owned and controlled by five transnational corporations, based in North America, which ranked among the most powerful in the world.

Although the bauxite industry may have been important as a provider of foreign exchange to the economy, it offered few other benefits. It made no impact, for example, on the chronic levels of unemployment in Jamaica. The ratio of capital to labour in the mining sector was, and still is, very high due to the capital-intensive nature of the industry. Thus, as one author, Owen Jefferson, wrote, 'In 1960, the value of fixed assets per man employed in the (mining) industry in Jamaica was US$33,817. For most sectors in manufacturing industry at this time, the equivalent figure ranged from US$1,096 to US$5,480'. In 1968, the industry employed only 5,000 workers and, while contributing as much as 10 per cent to the GDP, it accounted for a mere 0.8 per cent of the island's work-force. Indeed, the productivity of this sector was clearly illusrated in 1960, when the gross output per worker was J$9,236, while the equivalent figure for agricultural workers was a mere J$219.60. The contrast could hardly be more stark.

Despite the phenomenal growth in real GDP and the development of the productive forces — and in spite of the fact that, from 1950 to 1968, about 270,000 Jamaicans (and this figure for obvious reasons excludes tens of thousands of illegal immigrants) entered the United Kingdom, Canada and the United States — the rate of unemployment remained enormously high and increased quite dramatically (albeit unevenly) from 15 to 20 per cent in 1952 to 25 per cent in 1971.

From 1960 to 1968, while the rest of the economy was experiencing spectacular rates of growth, agriculture virtually stagnated and registered an annual growth rate of 3.2 per cent for the main export crops and 2.1 per cent in the production of crops for domestic consumption. As was to be expected in the circumstances, the food import bill increased dramatically, from US$26.85 million in 1950 to US$158.65 million in 1968. Even more alarming was the fact that the amount of food imported over the same period as a percentage of national consumption increased from 16.2 per cent to 32.2 per cent.

The underlying causes of the crisis in Jamaican agriculture are closely related to the extremely uneven distribution of land on the island and the pervasiveness of idle and under-utilised agricultural land on large estates. The agricultural census of 1968-69 indicated that 78.3 per cent of all Jamaican farms were those of less than five acres in area, while only 0.15 per cent of all farms were of more than 500 acres. These figures mean that 78.3 per cent of all farmers (a total of 151,705) occupy a mere 14.8 per cent of the land. In addition, one authority estimates that there are about 500,000 acres of idle land to be found on the large estates, out of a total of 1,508,000 acres of agricultural land.

A comparison of the agricultural and mining sector gives a clear indication of what Samir Amin has called 'disarticulated development'. While bauxite boomed, stimulating the manufacturing sector, agriculture was facing a deepening crisis. From 1950 to 1968, when mining's share of total investment was 17.2 per cent and that of manufacturing was 12.6 per cent, agriculture accounted for only 9 per cent. In 1968, manufacturing contributed 14.7 per cent to the GDP and employed 11.5 per cent of the labour force. Mining contributed 12.7 per cent to the GDP and employed a mere 0.8 per cent of the total labour force. Agriculture, however, contributed 9.9 per cent of the GDP and employed a disproportionately large 34.9 per cent of the total workforce of the island. In other words, more than a third of the labour force was concentrated in a sector which was declining in relative importance to the rest of the economy. Not surprisingly, with the relatively low level of investment in this sector and its resulting low level of productivity, the disparity of income between the sectors became even wider. Thus, while from 1957 to 1963, the lowest-paid workers in the mining sector received wage increases of 96 per cent, their counterparts in agriculture received a mere 31 per cent. In 1965, the average weekly wage of agricultural workers was J$7.80, while that of workers in mining was J$42.40.

This widening in income disparity can be seen in the economy as a whole during this period. In 1958 the top 10 per cent of income earners received 43.5 per cent of the total income of the island. By 1971, this figure had increased to 49.5 per cent. There was a corresponding fall in the income of the poorest 40 per cent of workers from 7.2 per cent to 5.4 per cent of total income. This resulted in rises in the levels of absolute poverty as the poorest 30 per cent of the population saw their weekly incomes fall from J$32 to J$25 between 1958 and 1968. By 1962, about 62 per cent of the labour force was earning less than J$20 a week.

This situation gave rise to growing social tension. The number of strikes increased from 37 in 1965 to 187 in 1970, and were accompanied by rising levels of violence on the streets. Against this background and in the face of mounting charges of political victimisation, corruption and police harassment, the government of Prime Minister Hugh Shearer was heavily defeated in the 1972 elections by Michael Manley's People's National Party (PNP) and its programme of 'democratic socialism'.

The PNP and the Manley Government

The People's National Party was founded in 1938 during the workers' and peasants' uprising of that year. At that time, it was dominated by middle-class professionals. However, this basis of support gradually shifted so that, by 1952, it had become as much a party of the Jamaican business class as a party of the less-privileged groups in Jamaican society. Members of Jamaica's business class held influential positions within the party itself. Eli Matalon, a member of one of the wealthiest Jamaican families was Minister of National Security in Manley's first cabinet (of 1972). Thus, there is a high degree of tension within the party between its apparent base of support among Jamaican workers and the wealthy leadership of the party, committed not to equality but to the sanctity of private property.

During the 1972 election campaign, the PNP never used the word 'socialism'. There was talk of 'popular participation' and 'social justice' but never was there any talk of socialism by Manley and his colleagues. Indeed, on coming to power, he reiterated time and again that he did not believe in 'isms'. In his recent book, however, Manley tells us that, at the first national executive committee meeting of his party after the victory of 1972, he urged his party to return to its socialist roots and re-examine systematically its ideology. The final product of this long process of self-reflection on the part of the party came in late 1974: the PNP declared to the public that its ideology was 'democratic socialism'. However, the document published by the party in November 1974, *Democratic Socialism: The Jamaican Model,* is more a declaration of principles than a call to action. The document reads:

'Socialism is first an ideal, a goal and an attitude of mind that requires people to care for each other's welfare. Socialism is a way of life. A Socialist Society cannot simply come into existence. It has to be built by people who believe and practise its principles.

Socialism is the Christian way of life in action. It is the philosophy that best gives expression to the Christian ideal of equality of all God's children. It has as its foundation the Christian belief that all men and women must love their neighbours as themselves'.

This good-intentioned but very vague formulation is characteristic of the whole document. Little or nothing is said about how this new society is to be achieved. It talks about the 'mixed economy' without really specifying what the mixture will be of the private and the public sectors. It speaks about the quest for equality, but at the same time clings to the importance of private property. The question of how this equality is to be achieved, without seriously challenging the profoundly unequal distribution of wealth and income based on the inequalities in the possession of private property, is not addressed in this pamphlet. Moreover, the PNP states quite categorically and indeed in italics, *'This Government rejects any form of expropriation'*. The document also made it quite clear that capitalists have a permanent place and role in the new democratic socialist Jamaica. All that they needed to do in their quest for profits was to be 'responsible' and operate 'within the bounds of the national interest and the rights of the people'. Foreign capital was promised a warm welcome and was 'assured a fair return on investment and fair and consistent treatment', provided that the investment was in accordance with the 'national interest' and the investor did not object if he or she was required to enter joint ventures with the state and/or Jamaican capital, and he or she was willing to operate in Jamaica on a basis of an undefined conception of 'good corporate citizenship'.

The Manley government reflected these vague formulations in its programme aimed to relieve the poverty and social tension the country was facing. His government initiated crash programmes to alleviate the chronic levels of unemployment. Free education was introduced, campaigns against illiteracy were inaugurated and a limited land reform programme was begun. The minimum voting age was lowered from 21 to 18 years, food subsidies were introduced, a national minimum wage level was set, the Rent Restriction Act was revised in favour of tenants and plans for worker participation in industry were also announced. In addition to these measures, several public utilities — such as electricity, certain sectors of public transport and the telephone services — were nationalised.

State expenditure increased dramatically. In 1970, public administration accounted for 8.4 per cent of the GDP. By 1974, that figure had almost doubled to 14.3 per cent. In 1962-63, there were 8,570 civil servants; in 1975 the number (excluding teachers, police and judges) was 15,570. Expenditure on education rose from J\$44.73 million in 1972-73 to J\$150.7 million in 1976-77. Similarly, government spending on agriculture rose from J\$34.8 million in 1972-73 to J\$105 million in 1976-77 as a result of the land reform and the extension of the co-operative system to the sugar industry. But the economy was unable to cope with such expenditures and the public debt soared. From 1972 to 1974 it increased by 56.7 per cent from J\$332.6 million to J\$520.8 million. More significantly, the percentage of foreign loans in the public debt over the same period increased by 75.6 per cent. In 1974 the foreign debt was equivalent to 48.9 per cent of government revenue. During the 1972-74 period, the Jamaican economy was adversely affected by the down-turn in the world economy, and the deteriorating terms of trade with the country's main partners. However, the straw which finally broke the back of the Jamaican economy was the spectactular 359 per cent increase in the price of crude oil, which increased Jamaica's import bill from J$44 million in 1972 to J$117 million in 1974. The crisis took a dramatic turn for the worse and drastic action was required to avert economic collapse.

In the face of such an adverse international situation, the government looked to the bauxite industry as a source of revenue to fund increased government expenditure. In mid-1974, the Bauxite Production Levy Act was passed. It obliged the bauxite producers to maintain production at 90 per cent of capacity, increased the tax rate on each ton produced and committed the government to greater participation in the industry by way of nationalisation or partnership with the producing companies.

For the first few years the bauxite levy paid handsome dividends as revenue per ton increased from J$2.50 to J$14.51. From 1972 to 1974 the revenue from the bauxite industry rocketed from J$22.7 million to an astronomical J$170.34 million, an increase of more than 650 per cent.

The offensive did not stop there. Inspired by the spectacular success of OPEC, in March 1974, Jamaica emerged as a leading light in the struggle to form the International Bauxite Association (IBA), which eventually came into being on 29 July 1975, with its headquarters in Kingston, Jamaica.

As was to be expected, the North American companies operating in the bauxite industry retaliated. They went to the International Centre for the Settlement of Investment Disputes to contest the legality of the levy. Bauxite production was drastically cut in Jamaica while the companies switched to other sources of supply. The US reduced its imports of Jamaican bauxite and one company, Revere, closed its Jamaican operations altogether. In concrete terms, this meant that, by 1976, the production of bauxite in Jamaica had fallen by 32.1 per cent from its 1974 level. State revenue from the bauxite industry accordingly fell, from J$170.34 million in 1974 to J$119.01 million in 1976. Jamaica's position in the league of bauxite producers deteriorated dramatically, reflecting the companies' switch of production out of Jamaica, particularly to Australia and Guinea Conakry. Jamaica's share of world production fell from 18.9 per cent in 1973 to 13.8 per cent in 1976, while Guinea increased its share from 3.9 per cent to 15 per cent.

Jamaica's other main export crop, sugar, also ran into difficulties at this time. In 1976, the sugar harvest failed because of an epidemic of smut and rust disease as well as a drought. At the same time, the world price of sugar plummeted. In June 1976, the price of sugar in Jamaica's largest market, the EEC, stood at £260 per tonne. By June 1977, the price had fallen to £188 per tonne.

The country's economic difficulties were compounded by the hostility of the United States to the Manley government. Relations reached a new low after Manley had supported the sending of Cuban troops to Angola in 1975. The US government launched a campaign to discourage tourists from visiting the island. Articles in the US press portrayed the country as dangerous and violent. In 1974, US visitors accounted for 78.4 per cent of the total number of tourists to the island. By 1976, this had fallen to 70 per cent. Receipts from tourism collected by the Bank of Jamaica fell from US$133.2 million in 1974 to US$71.7 million in 1977.

One of the problems of the Manley regime in its early years, especially after 1974, when the PNP declared its commitment to democratic socialism, was its use of fiery rhetoric far out of proportion to the concrete policies Manley was prepared to pursue. This rhetoric, together with the close ties established with Cuba greatly antagonised the wealthy Jamaicans but did nothing to curtail wealth and influence. The elite were thus able to undermine the government's economic plans by cutting production and spiriting capital out of the country. The first major wave of capital flight took place in 1976 and involved an estimated US$300 million. In addition, the rate of investment fell dramatically and there were large-scale redundancies. Members of the professional and upper classes began to leave the country in large numbers.

In 1976, Jamaica entered one of the bloodiest elections in its history. A right-wing coup attempt was foiled shortly before it could take place. Proof of US government involvement in an attempt to destabilise the Manley regime was provided by ex-US secret service agent Philip Agee, who visited the country in 1976 and identified 11 CIA agents in the US embassy in Kingston, and found evidence of their activities.

Despite these efforts however, Manley was re-elected with an increased majority. The poor had recognised the real gains they had made under the Manley government. But, despite this victory and Manley's determination to proceed with his democratic socialist alternative, Jamaica was starved by then of the foreign exchange needed to meet its balance of payments deficits. Negotiations with the IMF, which had begun shortly before the elections, now took centre stage.

The IMF and the Fall of the PNP

The disagreements between the IMF and the PNP regime, which came to the fore in July 1977, can be traced back to July 1974 when the IMF explicitly expressed its disquiet over certain aspects of government policy in Jamaica. In the annual staff consultation report, it referred to a wide range of policy issues, including wage increases, the fiscal deficit, monetary expansion and restrictions on trade and prices that it considered had contributed to Jamaica's problem. These private qualms were to become more widely aired as negotiations advanced.

The PNP government's call for IMF assistance was not caused solely by the pressures on the Jamaican economy. It was also a result of the government's own lack of alternative policies. The government was caught by the limits of its own self-imposed options. It was unwilling to seek a radical transformation of the Jamaican economy because this would have involved confrontation with the Jamaican capital-owning class. This was despite the result of the elections, which had given the government a strong mandate for such radical policies. The results showed a clear class polarisation, with the Jamaican capital-owning class and professional middle class voting with the conservative Jamaica Labour Party and the poor and working class voting for the PNP. The following results of a study, by the Jamaican political sociologist, Carl Stone, of the 1972 and 1976 general elections, shows this clearly:

	PNP vote 1972 (%)	PNP vote 1976 (%)
Unemployed and unskilled	52	60
Manual wage labour	61	72
White collar wage labour	75	57
Business and management class and high-income professionals	60	20
Farm labour	52	56
Small peasants	47	45

Source: 'Jamaica's 1980 Elections', *Caribbean Review,* Vol.x, No.2, 1981, p.40.

However, the PNP was unprepared to mobilise this base of support along an alternative path of development to that advocated by the IMF. In October 1976, negotiations with the IMF were postponed as the conditions demanded, such as a 40 per cent devaluation of the currency, were felt by Manley to be unacceptably harsh. Nevertheless, talks were resumed in December.

However, these negotiations soon ran into difficulties over the need for devaluation, over the extent of cuts in government expenditure which would be required, and over the incomes and wages policy that should be followed. The trade unions and radical forces in Jamaica would not agree to IMF demands so Manley and his cabinet had to break off discussions once again. Manley declared to the nation, on 5 January 1977: 'This government, on behalf of our people, will not accept anybody anywhere in the world telling us what to do in our country. We are the masters in our own house and in our house there shall be no other master but ourselves. Above all, we are not for sale'.

In early 1977, however, the Carter administration had taken office in the US. It promised to be more accommodating to the Manley regime than its hawkish predecessor had been. But one important condition would have to be met by the Jamaican government before the US would forward financial assistance — agreement would have to be reached with the IMF.

In April 1977, the Manley government announced its own austerity programme, which included an Emergency Production Plan, a six-month wage freeze and a new petrol tax. At the same time, emissaries of the government were sent in search of new sources of loans. Ministers visited Venezuela, Cuba and Trinidad and Tobago to borrow the money needed to cover the expected US$250 million imbalance in external payments. Because the government had not reached an agreement with the IMF, the international commercial banks refused to make any loans to the country. The PNP did not seriously explore the possibility of widening Jamaica's trade network to include the socialist countries until the crisis came to a head in early 1977. Only then did the government send representatives to seek loans from eastern Europe. By that time, it was clearly too late and Moscow, in any case, was reluctant to help. Manley was told bluntly to get aid from the culprits of his country's plight, the West.

The IMF Medicine

By mid-1977, the Manley government had run out of alternatives and, in July, an agreement with the IMF was finally signed. The results of this agreement for the majority of Jamaicans were catastrophic. In less than two years, the Jamaican dollar was devalued from an exchange rate of US$1.10 to US$0.56, a reduction of 49 per cent. The impact of this on Jamaica's open economy which is highly dependent on imported goods, was a rapid rise in the cost of living: the consumer

EXCHANGE RATE ADJUSTMENTS 1973-1979

Date	Revised Rate	% Change
17.1.73	J$1.00 = US$1.10	15.6
24.4.77	Basic: J$1.00 = US$1.10	
	Special: J$1.00 = US$0.80	−27.3
24.10.77	Basic: J$1.00 = US$1.10	
	Special: J$1.00 = US$0.78	−2.5
13.1.78	Basic: J$1.00 = US$0.95	−13.6
	Special: J$1.00 = US$0.74	−5.1
9.5.78	J$1.00 = US$0.645	−47.3
		−14.7
9.6.78	J$1.00 = US$0.636	−1.5
13.7.78	J$1.00 = US$0.626	−1.5
10.8.78	J$1.00 = US$0.617	−1.5
14.9.78	J$1.00 = US$0.608	−1.5
12.10.78	J$1.00 = US$0.602	−1.0
9.11.78	J$1.00 = US$0.595	−1.0
7.12.78	J$1.00 = US$0.589	−1.0
8.1.79	J$1.00 = US$0.584	−1.0
12.2.79	J$1.00 = US$0.578	−1.0
12.3.79	J$1.00 = US$0.572	−1.0
9.4.79	J$1.00 = US$0.566	−1.0
7.5.79	J$1.00 = US$0.560	−1.0

Source: National Planning Agency (Jamaica), Economic and Social Survey 1979.

price index jumped from an annual increase of 14.1 per cent in 1977 to a phenomenal 49.9 per cent in 1978. The price of food and drink alone increased in 1978 by 54.1 per cent. Real wages fell in 1978 by as much as 35 per cent in some sectors. The rate of unemployment, which stood at 24.6 per cent in April 1977, increased to an all-time high of 31.1 per cent by October 1979.

According to the calculations of the Department of Statistics published in 1981, real disposable income per capita by 1980 had fallen to 1967 levels. From 1974 to 1980, there was a decline in the actual consumption of basic items, such as food (by 31.3 per cent), non-alcoholic beverages (by 76.7 per cent), clothing and footwear (by 59.3 per cent), furniture, furnishings and household equipment (by 22.5 per cent).

Behind the IMF measures was the assumption that the Jamaican government would encourage foreign investment at the same time as it would provide security and incentives to local business people. However, foreign capital kept its distance from the island. In June 1978, the international commercial banks agreed to re-finance only seven-eighths of Jamaica's debts as they fell due and refused to make any additional loans. Domestic capital owners also refused to invest. Gross capital investment, as a percentage of GDP stood at 35.1 per cent in 1969 but fell to 12.5 per cent in 1977. The bulk of investment during this period was in fact carried out by the state, as it was evident that Jamaica was facing a virtual investment strike. At the same time, capital continued to flow out of the country, legally and illegally. Private net capital outflows were J$5.1 million in 1975. By 1978, this drip had turned into a veritable flood, reaching J$145.8 million, about 28 times the 1975 figure.

It was clear that the IMF recipes were not working even in their own terms. Michael Manley said as much in his address to the 1979 annual meeting of the Board of Governors of the Inter-American Development Bank: 'We have found that, having met all the terms and conditions which the situation demanded, and having worked to mobilise the nation to rise to the central challenge of production, we continued nevertheless to stagnate . . . It was as if the medicine could arrest the disease, but the diet could not provide the foundation for recovery'.

In December 1979, Jamaica failed to meet the international reserve targets laid down by the IMF. Sixty per cent of the shortfall in foreign exchange reserves was due to factors beyond the country's control. Floods in 1979 had destroyed US$20 million worth of export crops, an increase in the cost of oil imports had added US$33 million to the import bill. International inflation was higher than IMF projections, adding US$18 million to the import bill and a sharp rise in interest rates added a further US$31 million.

The IMF ignored these extenuating factors and refused to allow Jamaica to continue drawing credit from the Fund. Furthermore, it laid down even harsher conditions for the credit facility to be reactivated. It demanded a major reorganisation of the structure of state administration, a trimming and streamlining of the public sector and sweeping cuts in public expenditure. Of these, the last was the most devastating and draconian. The Fund demanded a J$300 million reduction in state expenditure in the financial year 1980-81. Manley and his collegues would have had to implement 50 per cent of this reduction (J$150 million) before the IMF would agree to disregard the failed December 1979 performance tests. This would have meant a J$50 million cut in the wage bill of central government through the dismissal of 11,000 public sector workers. Moreover, despite the implications of such a step in a country with very high levels of unemployment, the IMF waiver would only entitle Jamaica to one tranche of credit, a mere US$30 million. The release of the remaining tranches would be conditional on Jamaica taking resolute action to achieve the remaining J$150 million reduction in state expenditure. The fund also made clear that it would not augment the lending programme to take account of higher import prices and interest rates.

The response of the PNP government, however, was only further appeasement of the IMF, the motive of its entire encounter with that institution. The number of cabinet ministries was reduced from 21 to 14; auditing and management improvements in the state-owned enterprises were accepted; the government also agreed to invite local businessmen to lease some state-owned hotels and some state-owned land, the latter in order, it was claimed, to increase the production of export crops. Although the drastic reduction in the budget was somewhat unpalatable to the PNP, in the end, Manley and his colleagues conceded an immediate cut of J$100 million. However, pressure from the trade union movement forced the government to refuse the extra J$50 million which the IMF had demanded, in order to save 11,000 public sector jobs. Despite the big concessions the government had made the IMF refused to modify its initial position.

Nine months later, at the 35th annual meeting of the Board of Governors of the IMF, held in Washington in the autumn of 1980, Jamaica's Minister of Finance Hugh Small made an ingenious but vain attempt to bring home to the bureaucrats of the IMF what their measures meant for Jamaica:

'According to our calculations, if the United States was asked to make an 'adjustment' of this relative magnitude, it would need to reduce the federal budget for 1980-81 by some US$103 billion. There would also have to be retrenchment of some 1,700,000 employees from the federal and state administrations. We cannot think of any better way to dramatise the *assymetry of adjustment* and the problem of *conditionality* as it affects the developing countries, in real human terms.' (author's emphasis).

The IMF, was, as usual, totally impervious to this plea. Indeed, it rejected the PNP's entreaties by curtly dismissing Jamaica as merely another ungrateful 'spoilt child'! (*sic*). Its own evaluation of its treatment of Jamaica given in an official document illustrates its view of the situation:

'An objective evaluation of the Fund's role in Jamaica must conclude that the Fund had been generous in terms of financial and technical support; co-operative in efforts to mobilise assistance from other external sources; liberal as regards the time allowed for the adjustment of demand; mindful of the external shocks and mishaps over which Jamaica has had no control; and sensitive to the social and political realities of the country'.

The IMF sincerely holds such views and, moreover, by its yardstick, it was, in fact, 'generous' to the Manley regime. It taxes the brain to imagine what the IMF does when in a parsimonious mood!

In any case, the National Executive Committee of the PNP, at its famous 22 March 1980 meeting, rejected the IMF proposals by a margin of two to one. This has often been recorded by commentators. However, what has been seldom reported is the fact that, along with Eric Bell, the Minister of Finance (who resigned two days after this meeting) and his Minister of State, Richard Fletcher, Michael Manley urged the PNP to accept the IMF conditions and voted for their acceptance by the party.

On one level this shows the inconsistencies and demagogy of Manley: in the public domain he was very outspoken against the IMF, but when it came to the crunch, behind closed doors, he buckled under its pressures.

On another level, however, it illustrates a certain consistency in Manley's practice, since he realised that the pre-condition to any alternative to IMF policies was a radical transformation of power relations in Jamaica. The government would have had to contemplate the expropriation of the 500,000 acres of idle land held by Jamaica's powerful landowning class. Instead of pleading with and bribing businessmen to keep the factories open, the PNP would have had to seriously consider the possibility of the workers taking over these factories to save their jobs and protect their livelihood.

The PNP never considered such a radical rupture of social relations within Jamaica. Since its birth, during the working class and peasant uprisings of 1938, the PNP has always been a party dominated and financed (albeit somewhat inconspicuously) by middle-class professionals and, since 1952, by a powerful section of the Jamaican business class. Reliable sources claim that, even in the run-up to the October 1980 elections, one of Jamaica's most powerful families and long-standing supporters of the PNP donated J$100,000 to the impoverished party. Furthermore, although most leading members of the PNP have been members of the liberal professions, its programmes and policies have reflected the party's role as defender of Jamaica's capitalists.

The PNP is, by its nature, unable to challenge the capitalist system in Jamaica and effect radical social change. This helps explain the party's capitulation to the IMF. But the PNP faced a huge dilemma. It was unwilling to seek a radical transformation of society, but nor could it win over Jamaica's business class to its policies. Frightened by the PNP's rhetoric and its mass following, business people refused to invest in the country. Although the PNP government gave unprecedented subsidies to industry and pursued an alliance with local

98

capitalists, this was to no avail. Factories were left idle and workers were made redundant. Despite all this the PNP made no attempt to deal with what was, in effect, economic sabotage in a bid to bring down the government. There was no attempt to nationalize companies which were refusing to co-operate with government plans and 80 per cent of the economy remained in private hands.

It was this impasse between Jamaica's capitalist class and the Manley government which resulted in the balance of payments crisis and the country's economic ruin. With all radical options foreclosed, IMF recipes emerged by default as the only option for the PNP, the only way to break the deadlock. However, the prescriptions of the IMF, as we have seen, spelt disaster for the Jamaican urban and rural poor. Thus, in the end, Manley managed to alienate not just the dominant classes, but also the working class and oppressed who had to suffer the consequences of IMF policies. It was therefore not at all surprising that, in the elections of 30 October 1980, Jamaicans voted Manley out and placed in power the right-wing Jamaican Labour Party of Edward Seaga.

The Manley Period in Retrospect

'The masses of Jamaica are not for sale', declared Manley to an overflowing and cheering crowd at the National Stadium in Kingston on 19 September 1976. 'Above all', Manley reminded the Jamaican people on 5 January 1977, 'we are not for sale'. But in fact, under the Manley government, Jamaica succumbed to the IMF's demands. Nevertheless, despite the government's acceptance of IMF austerity measures, they failed to work. From mid-1978 to March 1980, Jamaica fulfilled all the requirements of the IMF programme, but the economy did not recover. Real GDP fell by 2 per cent in 1977, 1.7 per cent in 1978, 2.2 per cent in 1979 and 5.3 per cent in 1980. From 1976 to 1980, manufacturing output declined in real terms by 34.8 per cent.

The failure of the IMF policies is a reflection of the way the Fund had diagnosed the Jamaican problem. The IMF diagnosis of the country's balance of payments difficulties suggested that exports had been reduced and imports increased by the government's wage policy. On the import side, the IMF suggested that the value of imports had increased as a consequence of excessive consumption generated by the increase in wages and an excessive deficit in the government's budget, which it financed by expanding the money supply. The IMF claimed that wage rises generated higher costs, which eroded the competitiveness of Jamaican exports on the world market.

But the evidence does not support the IMF conclusions. The

99

increase in the country's import bill for instance, had very little to do with an increase in the volume of imports. Rather it was a reflection of the increase in the cost of imported items, which was being generated by an inflationary spiral in the capitalist world economy at the time. In fact, from 1972 (the year the PNP came into office) to 1976 (the year of the Jamaican crisis), while the volume (i.e. the actual quantity) of imported items experienced a cumulative decline of 31.3 per cent, the value of these same items increased by 65.4 per cent. Nor is it true that excessive wage increases were responsible for the erosion of the competitiveness of Jamaican exports. During this period, there were substantial increases in real wages. Indeed, from 1973 to 1976, real average wages had increased by 28.9 per cent, an increase which had markedly improved the quality of life of the Jamaican working class. But these wage increases arose from a very low base. The average weekly income in October 1976 was a mere J$27 (at that time J$1 was worth about £0.50), while the national minimum wage stood at J$20. In 1973, the average weekly income stood at an abysmally low J$12. Therefore, it is clear that the wage increases during the early 1970s, though significant in relative terms, were far less significant when one takes into account their absolute values.

Jamaica's principal export commodities, bauxite, alumina, sugar and bananas, accounted for 83 per cent of the island's exports in 1973 and 1974. The bauxite and alumina industry, which alone accounted for 71 per cent of Jamaica's export earnings in 1974, experienced a big decline in output in the two subsequent years. This was partly due to the recession in the world economy, especially in the United States, which was by far the largest market for Jamaican ore, and partly due to the switch to Australian and Guinean ore. This switch, according to the bauxite companies, was a reaction to the lack of competitiveness of Jamaican ore. However, the companies could not snipe at wage levels in claiming a lack of competitiveness, but rather were aiming at the Bauxite Production Levy Act of 1974.

In that year, the transnational corporations operating within the bauxite enclave paid taxes of J$144 million, compared to only J$21.07 million in 1973. This was a direct consequence of the levy. The cost of local salaries and wages amounted to a relatively small J$55 million. In fact wage costs in the industry in 1974 comprised a mere 11.5 per cent of the declared value of bauxite and alumina exports, itself an underestimation of the true value of those exports. The idea that wage increases could account for the fall in competitiveness of Jamaican bauxite therefore, is not supported by the evidence.

The two other main Jamaican exports, sugar and bananas, had fixed export quotas for the EEC and North American markets, with negotiated prices denominated in foreign currency. Jamaica failed to fulfil its quotas in 1975 and 1976, but all concerned were agreed that the underlying causes of these failures were not wage increases, but the old technological and organisational backwardness of these sectors. Also in 1976, Jamaica's sugar crop, as has been noted above, was afflicted by diseases.

Manufacturing and certain sectors of agriculture made up the only exports which operated on a relatively open market. But such products account for less than 20 per cent of Jamaica's total exports, and moreover, imported raw materials, not wages, are the most costly element in the manufacturing sector. Indeed, according to one study in 1977, imported raw materials accounted for no less than 39 per cent of the gross value of production of selected manufactures, while wage costs amounted to a relatively small 21 per cent. It is obvious that wage increases here would invariably push up costs. But, when one takes into account the relatively small proportion of production costs which the wage bill comprised, and the fact that the non-traditional exports accounted for a relatively small percentage of total exports, it becomes clear that the argument that wage increases explain the balance of payments crisis of the Jamaican economy at the end of 1976 does not stand up. In the crisis years, 1975 and 1976, it was not this non-traditional sector of the economy which registered reductions in exports, but rather the traditional bauxite/alumina and agricultural sectors.

Not only, therefore, were the prescriptions of the IMF disastrous for the Jamaican people, its diagnosis of the Jamaican problem was also fundamentally flawed. So, as Girvan, Bernal and Hughes wrote, there is much in the analysis and methodology of the IMF 'which one could find amusing from the intellectual standpoint, were it not that so much damage has been caused by the imposition of policy measures which assume the validity of the diagnosis'.

The experience of the encounter of the PNP regime with the IMF leads us to the following conclusions:

i. The diagnosis of, and the prescriptions proffered by the IMF for the alleviation of the balance of payments problems of Third World governments — especially those committed to reform rather than radical change — end in disaster. Instead of a cure, IMF medicine exacerbates the illness of the patient not only socially but (assuming for the moment that we can distinguish between the two) economically as well.

ii. For Third World regimes committed to reform, acceptance of IMF policies means the abandonment, and indeed reversal, of the various reforms being implemented. Living standards fell dramatically under the Manley government. The real average weekly income of those fortunate enough to find employment declined by 52 per cent from April 1975 to November 1980.

iii. The IMF is not, as it maintains, 'above politics'. During sensitive negotiations with the PNP regime in Jamaica, for instance, the IMF held meetings with Edward Seaga, the opposition leader, and his colleagues, and divulged to the latter confidential details of its talks with Manley. It is also by no means far-fetched to say that, by the end of 1979, the IMF had hardened its position during the negotiations to facilitate the early fall of Manley in the light of the PNP's growing unpopularity in Jamaica. Ironically, this unpopularity of the government was largely due to the hardship caused by the PNP's adherence to the very measures proposed by the IMF itself. The second and more fundamental sense in which the IMF is politically biased is in the overall thrust of its policies when it encounters reform-oriented regimes. Its objective is to realign the government's policies according to a defined package of economic and political priorities suited to the needs of western capitalist nations. Thus the IMF demanded wage freezes, the end of price controls, redundancies, de-regulation of the economy, a *de facto* minimum guaranteed rate of return on capital and cuts in redistributive state expenditure. In short, these demands represented a series of measures which shifted the balance of power away from labour and in favour of capital, and undermined any commitment to social justice and redistribution of wealth.

iv. Although it is generally thought that an agreement with the IMF is a 'seal of approval' which enables the country concerned to borrow from international commercial banks, in Jamaica's case, this was far from being the truth. Despite the several agreements struck by the IMF with the PNP regime, from 1976 and especially after the first failure to agree in 1977, the commercial banks were extremely reluctant to reschedule debts and flatly refused to provide the PNP regime with new loans.

v. We should not blame the IMF for the fall of Michael Manley, except perhaps in the most immediate sense, because the IMF's activities in Jamaica, far from being aberrations, were totally in character with its previous treatment of similar regimes. Therefore, such actions by the IMF should have been expected. Blame resides more with the PNP itself, which refrained from taking adequate actions to deal with Jamaica's long and conspicuous crisis. The primary factor which led to the government's turn to the IMF was the fall in production in both agriculture and industry. This began as early as 1974 when Jamaican business people made it clear that they would not invest. Closures and redundancies increased. The PNP had two choices — either to abandon its promises of reform and its radical rhetoric or, especially after its massive mandate of 1976, to change power relations radically in Jamaica. The latter policy in conjunction with a concerted diversification of trade relations to break Jamaican dependence on the US economy would have offered some hope for the majority of Jamaicans. As it turned out, the standard of living of that majority could hardly have deteriorated more than it did at the behest of the IMF.

The IMF and 'Deliverance'

'Deliverance is near' — Jamaican Labour Party slogan in the 1980 general election. 'For God has sent us a deliverer, who is going to deliver us out of this wicked Babylon'. 'All we need in this time is deliverance'. — Lyrics from two of the JLP's campaign songs.

With the staccato sound of M16 rifles still echoing in the streets of Kingston, the JLP won a landslide victory in the 1980 general election. The election was marked by unprecedented levels of violence and terror, and it soon became clear that the promised deliverance and the path to the New Jerusalem was to be provided by the operation of unencumbered market forces.

The economic programme of the JLP coincided exactly with the views of the IMF. In fact, negotiations between the two had effectively begun in June 1980, a full four months before the election. Long before they took office, therefore, Seaga and his colleagues were quite clear what the IMF expected, if the loans the new government needed were to be forthcoming. The JLP acted accordingly and the institutional framework for the realization of the strategy of export-oriented growth, the Puerto Rican model, was rapidly moved into place.

Opening the economy to foreign competition and reducing state spending began immediately. Public employees were laid off in their hundreds. Privatization of nationalized industries began and many state entities were closed down or reduced in size. Restrictions on foreign trade and tariff barriers, behind which Jamaican farmers and industrial producers had developed their output, were removed as both agricultural and consumer goods flooded into the country. The result was the alienation of small farmers, unions and local producers from the Seaga policies.

In April 1981, an agreement was signed with the IMF. Over a three-year period, Jamaica was allocated US$650 million from the Extended

103

Fund Facility and US$48 million from the Compensatory Fund Facility.

The conditions imposed by the IMF did not appear to be onerous. No devaluation was demanded, no more redundancies in the public sector were called for and no curtailment in government programmes was needed. In addition, the IMF assistance was to be 'front loaded' — that is, Jamaica was to be permitted to draw 40 per cent of funds in the first year of the programme, compared with the more usual 30 per cent in the first year of an agreement. This meant that Jamaica would be entitled to US$308 million in the 12 months to March 1982.

However, to ensure that the government stayed on course, the IMF laid down certain conditions. Domestic bank credit to the public sector was limited so that funds would remain available for the private sector, inflation was to be reduced by the control of bank credit to the economy, foreign exchange reserves were to be increased as exports dropped, foreign borrowing by the government was to be limited, and there were to be no currency restrictions introduced that would hinder the ability of either the government or the private sector to meet its overseas commitments.

Seaga, who is minister of finance and minister of mining as well as prime minister, proudly proclaimed to the Jamaican parliament that the deal was 'positive' for the local economy: 'It does not contain provision for devaluation of the Jamaican dollar, (nor) cutbacks in public sector employment or curtailment of specific programmes. All these were features of the previous agreements between the IMF and the government of Jamaica'. But then came the bad news for Jamaican wage-earners. For those employed in the public sector, Seaga explained,

'To maintain current expenditure, wage restraint in the public sector is inevitable inasmuch as compensation to employees accounts for 76 per cent of every dollar of revenue. The public sector, therefore, and public enterprises supported by the budget, will be subjected to a three-year pay plan'.

This plan was to result in the reduction of the real income of public sector workers. It based pay increases, not on the movement of prices as Manley had attempted during his period of office, but rather on 'the availability of budgetary resources.' Needless to say, the budgetary resources were strictly limited by the government and the IMF.

As for the workers in the private sector, the government, in its memorandum to the IMF, after pointing out that 'employers and employees should settle pay claims by free negotiation', effectively qualified this stipulation out of existence when it stated, 'parties to

104

industrial disputes should be encouraged to settle claims based on the ability of the enterprise to pay, having regard to the implications for production costs and prices, the generation of company earnings for investment in production expansion and the creation of employment opportunities'. As the Workers' Party of Jamaica asked: 'Which employers ever state that they have the ability to pay higher wages?'

In addition, the government made quite clear that it intended to increase its powers of compulsory and binding arbitration. To back up this move, the chief of staff of the Jamaican Defence Force had pointed out that the army was ready to deal with any workers involved in industrial disputes. As one policeman told a group of striking workers: 'It's management's time now'. In addition to the *de facto* wage restraint, no less than half of the items that were on the government's price control list, implemented by the Manley regime, were removed. As was to be expected, the prices of these items increased sharply.

It has been suggested that the conditions demanded of the Seaga regime by the IMF were generous. Such a judgment fails to understand the nature of the relationship between the Fund and the Seaga government. Nor do the terms of the agreement reflect the financial wizardry that the prime minister was supposed to have exhibited during the negotiations. Rather, the terms of the Jamaican agreement are based upon the traditional logic of the IMF. Take, for example, the question of cuts in public expenditure and the resulting unemployment that such cuts produce. Three reasons can be suggested as to why the IMF did not demand such reductions in state employment. First, from November 1980 to April 1981, the Seaga regime had already made inroads into public sector employment. Most notably among these was the disbandment of the Youth Employment Scheme, which meant the shedding of 12,500 workers from the state's wage bill. Thus, Seaga had already done the dirty work for the IMF. Secondly, as Jennifer Ffrench pointed out in the *Weekly Gleaner* of 6 May 1981, to have demanded such reductions at such an early stage of the new government's period of office would have been asking 'the new administration to commit political suicide'. This would clearly have been against the interests of the IMF. Thirdly, implicit in the limitations placed on public spending was the shedding of more jobs in the future. There was no need to make this explicit and thus evoke public opposition.

As far as devaluation was concerned, by the time the IMF agreement was signed in April 1981, the Jamaican dollar had been devalued by more than 60 per cent from the level four years before. The problem of the 'over-valued exchange rate', as Ffrench rightly noted, was no longer an issue.

Last and most important, the apparently favourable IMF conditions were granted to Jamaica precisely because the economic perspectives of Seaga and his colleagues coincided with those of the IMF. Both believed in the de-regulation of the economy so that market forces could have full rein. Both accepted the need for wage restraint while prices were allowed to rise without hindrance. Both agreed that state intervention in the economy should be kept to a minimum. Such a coincidence of economic perspectives, compared to the open hostility that characterised the Manley regime's relations with the Fund, is far more important in understanding the nature of the IMF conditions imposed on Jamaica than any idea of IMF generosity.

Since the IMF agreement was signed the performance of the Jamaican economy has not improved, as compared to its performance during the Manley years. Certain aspects, in fact, have been worse.

There were, however, some early successes. In 1981, real GDP increased by 3.3 per cent, which broke a run of six years of falling GDP. Inflation declined from an annual rate of 28.2 per cent in 1980 to 6.2 per cent in 1982. At current prices, investment in fixed capital has increased from a rate of minus 7.8 per cent in 1980 to 37.8 per cent in 1981 with further increases in 1982. By IMF standards, these results look impressive. Moreover, for the first two years of the IMF agreement, the Jamaican economy passed all the IMF quarterly performance tests. However, these macro-economic figures and success in achieving IMF targets give no indication about the welfare of the Jamaican people. They say nothing about employment or the standard of living of the majority of Jamaican people.

When Seaga came into office in November 1980, unemployment was running at 26.8 per cent of the labour force. By October 1981, it had declined to 25.6 per cent. However, by October 1982, the official figure had risen to 27.9 per cent. Furthermore, bad though the official figures are, there are claims that they have been manipulated by the government to cover up the severity of unemployment. Indeed, an article in *Business Week* in October 1982 quoted a trade union leader as saying: 'It must be the new math they are using to come up with these figures. It just doesn't add up to what we see'. Economists of the Workers' Party of Jamaica estimated unemployment in 1982 as one third of the labour force. Figures for certain sections of the workforce, notably women and young workers (those under 29 years old) are even more revealing. By October 1982, no less than 40.2 per cent of women and 44.6 per cent of young workers were unemployed.

Even those still in work continued to suffer falling living standards. Average incomes, which have fallen by over 50 per cent between 1974 and 1980, fell by a further 6.2 per cent in the two subsequent years. As government investment in social services and welfare payments were also falling, it is clear that the lot of the average Jamaican worker is deteriorating rapidly.

Even before the IMF deal was struck by Seaga in April 1981, loans had begun to flow into the country. Within the first five months of the JLP government, the country had received more foreign loans than the Manley regime received in the whole of its final year in office. A large percentage of the foreign currency received was spent on the import of consumer goods which flooded the market and undermined domestic producers. Importers were making large profits while local producers, as early as May 1981, were facing bankruptcy. The Jamaican Manufacturers Association (JMA) declared that the free flow of foreign goods into the domestic market 'meant the death knell for local industry'. Thus, the very producers who were meant to lead the export drive were being forced out of business.

The situation facing local producers did not improve in the subsequent months. In a remarkably frank pronouncement, Mr A. Anthony Williams, the President of the JMA declared 'Manufacturers demand that those riding on their back get off . . .' and that his members were no longer prepared to take 'the licks (blows) while others were laughing all the way to the bank'. It was clear that those laughing all the way to the bank were local importers who had made a killing when import restrictions were lifted, and the banks themselves. Between March 1982 and March 1983, the nine largest banks (seven of which are foreign controlled) had increases in pre-tax profits of 125 per cent. One bank in particular, the Eagle Merchant Bank announced a massive 600 per cent increase in its assets after only one year of operation. It is interesting to note that the Chairman of that bank was Mr Ossie Harding, the JLP Senate President and a major shareholder is Paul Chen Young, a close economic adviser of Prime Minister Seaga (*Struggle,* 25 April 1983).

The new private investments that have been received have generated a mere 3,000 of the 90,000 new jobs that the Seaga government promised it would create by 1984. Nor had the celebrated Caribbean Basin Initiative much to offer Jamaica. Of a total of US$350 million allocated for the scheme, Jamaica received only US$50 million in aid. Furthermore, the supposed opening up of the US market to Caribbean products will affect a miniscule 3 per cent of the exports of the region.

Thus, despite the plans and promises of the Seaga government and their IMF backers, the Jamaican economy continues to stagnate. Bauxite production has fallen to its lowest levels since the 1960s and the country's visible trade deficit increased by 47.6 per cent in 1982. The Jamaican dollar has been effectively devalued by the introduction

107

of a parallel market for foreign exchange. This means that many importers have to buy US dollars at a parallel rate of up to J$3.50 to the US dollar as compared with the official exchange rate of J$1.78 to the US dollar. This has considerably increased the costs of many imported items.

The outcome of the country's growing economic crisis was reflected in April 1983 when it failed to meet the IMF performance tests and its allotted US$160 million of Fund resources were frozen. Further austerity measures in the form of cuts in government spending, reducing imports by a further US$150 million, taxation increases and price increases encouraged the IMF to waive the failure of the performance tests and allow the country to draw another US$40 million immediately. Despite this however, Jamaica is finding it increasingly difficult to borrow from international commercial banks as servicing its US$2.3 billion external debt gets more expensive. Furthermore, direct foreign investment is also falling and many investment proposals are being withdrawn as the crisis deepens. As the foreign debt grows, to rival that of Mexico on a per capital basis, and US military aid to the regime expands alarmingly to counter the rising levels of social tension on the island, Jamaica's future could not be more uncertain.

Conclusion

Since the first IMF loan was granted in 1977, the social condition of the mass of the Jamaican people has markedly deteriorated and the economy has cumulatively declined. However, the social and economic crises of contemporary Jamaica cannot be simply 'blamed' on the IMF as many have tended to do. What can be said however, is that unviable economic measures were prescribed by the IMF, but were not executed by it. The measures were put into effect by the indigenous Jamaican ruling class, albeit not under circumstances totally within its control. It is nevertheless, undoubtedly the case that the economic medicine prescribed by the IMF, has, even by the latter's own limited criteria of 'success', palpably failed in Jamaica. Indeed, the effects of the IMF measures upon the vast majority of the Jamaican people have been far more disastrous than the calamities of droughts and floods that nature has seen fit to inflict upon them in recent years.

7 Proposals for Reform

'Whatever in fact happens to interest rates or to Latin American trade, the debt is now so huge that it devours all improvement, requiring still bigger improvement the following year. The debt is a black hole, growing large on the money it absorbs. Far from being the main symptom of the Latin American malaise, the debt has become the malaise itself.'

The Economist, April 1983

The effects of IMF stabilization programmes on the poor and underprivileged of the Third World have led to repeated calls for fundamental changes in the way it operates. On the other hand, the threat posed by the present debt crisis to the international financial community has led to proposals for IMF reform from Western bankers and policymakers. There are widely different objectives behind these calls for reform of the IMF.

Ringmaster of the International Banks

The concern of the Western financial establishment is to ensure that deficit nations continue to meet their commitments to Western banks. The present crisis has underlined the importance of the IMF to the financial community in achieving this objective and thus guaranteeing the stability of the financial system as a whole. The *Financial Times* remarked recently: 'The Fund is generally conceded to be the main remaining pillar propping up the world banking system and sustaining hope that general depression can be prevented from deteriorating into all-out recession. It has overtly emerged as ringmaster of the major international banks'. Yet there is still no unanimity of view on how the IMF should exercise this role.

109

The hard-line, free market view suggests that bailing out the debtor nations amounts to little less than the socialization of their losses by forcing Western taxpayers to pay for the extravagance of LDC governments. Furthermore, 'improvised, piecemeal rescue packages to protect debtor nations from financial collapse could lead to renewed world inflation and are a waste of resources', according to Professor Karl Brunner of the University of Rochester, New York. He argues that the debt crisis will be resolved by the operation of market forces and that the predicted upturn in the world economy will enable LDCs to meet their debt commitments. He does, however, concede that IMF resources could be increased 'temporarily' to meet the present severe liquidity crisis, but he warns that any permanent increase would be inflationary and would thus reduce the possibility of future growth. As far as the banks are concerned, as it is their own imprudence that has led to the present crisis, they will just have to accept the losses any LDC default will imply.

However, a more moderate view appears to have gained the agreement of most Western decision-makers. This view suggests that leaving the banks to accept heavy losses due to LDC default would place too great a strain on the international financial system. Thus, to enable LDCs to get back on course, a large and permanent increase in IMF resources is called for. Any inflationary pressure that this entails, it is argued, is outweighed by the unacceptable implications of bank collapses under the burden of LDC defaults. The IMF has agreed therefore, a major increase in quota payments (although not all member governments have the approval of their respective legislatures to pay the increases as yet). The increase will give the IMF nearly 50 per cent extra usable funds by the end of 1983. It has also borrowed from member states to increase the GAB to US$1.7 billion. Finally, there are suggestions that the IMF should borrow from the international financial market if it requires still more funds. All these extra resources, when taken up by debtor nations, will enable them to repay the bridging loans they received from the various central banks in the early days of the crisis and to reduce the level of private bank lending to LDCs to a more manageable proportion of their total debt.

Furthermore, it is being suggested that regulation of the private banks, either by the IMF or by their own central banks, is essential if the present crisis is not to be repeated. This could include forcing the banks to agree to country lending limits for their LDC customers, ensuring that extra reserves are put aside to cover possible bad debts, and that loan periods are extended and interest rates reduced. However, because all these measures would affect their profitability, they are being vigorously contested by the banks. For their own part, the banks are trying to improve their ability to predict a country's future capacity to repay its loans. To this end 35 US, European and Japanese banks have recently founded the Institute of International Finance to collect data on debtor nations and report to its member banks. It is planned to offer the services of the institute to hundreds of banks throughout the world. There are also discussions of ways in which private banks might better co-ordinate their actions when major rescheduling of bank debt is under discussion. A 'Paris Club' for private bankers has been mentioned.

Despite these efforts by the banks, the IMF faces the charge that its extra resources will do little more than help the private banks out of a corner of their own making. *The New York Times* reported potential congressional opposition from both right and left to the call to increase the US quota contribution to the IMF by US$8.4 billion. Some congressmen see only a bail-out for bankers and demand that they be made to suffer for their sins. They argue that the IMF is effectively taking taxpayers' money from around the world and using it to increase the profits of the private banks. Even Johannes Witteveen, a former managing director of the IMF, has admitted: 'We lent them (various governments) the money, but instead of staying in the country, the private banks got all their interest out and some got out their capital as well'. In fact, capital flight from Latin America to the US and Europe during 1981 and 1982 was estimated to be no less than US$10 billion as profits and the proceeds from liquidated assets were moved out of the region.

Various schemes have been suggested to force the banks to accept losses as a result of over-lending, and at the same time increase their liquidity and thus relax the pressure on the banking system. These would involve the banks selling their outstanding LDC loans at a discount to the IMF or the central banks. The difference between the actual value of the loan and the discount price received would be recorded as a loss in the banks' accounts. Yet, at the same time, the banks would have money available both to meet any demand from depositors who wished to withdraw their money from the bank for fear of a bank collapse, or to re-lend to their LDC customers. Thus the banking system would be protected while individual banks were forced to lower their profits.

The response of the banking community to a scheme that would reduce their profits has been predictable. One US banker was quoted in the *International Herald Tribune* as saying: 'No-one (in the banking community) wants their money back. It would only have to be re-lent. And at least we're earning a sensible margin on it. Why should I take a loss? My bank is not squeezed for liquidity. Yes, we've lost the flexibility about where we might have directed the repayments, had they been made, but we're earning more money'.

The Debt Crisis is Over, If Ever There was One!

It has been suggested that the country-by-country debt rescheduling operation, the increase in IMF resources and the general economic upswing that is now occurring, plus a helping of luck and 'fast footwork', have between them resolved the debt crisis problem. However, this view is hard to substantiate.

The long-awaited recovery in the world economy may not bring the expected relief to LDCs. It is estimated that a sustained period of economic growth of nearly 3 per cent a year would be necessary to produce the extra income LDCs need to pay their debts. Yet even that level of growth has so far not been attained and present growth could, as Dr Witteveen suggests, 'come to an untimely end'. Many LDCs, and particularly those in Latin America, are reported to be entering a down-turn and, according to the World Bank, their economic prospects are 'difficult' despite a mild up-turn in the West. 'There is a very real danger', states Mr Tom Clausen, president of the World Bank, 'that the deepening recession in the Third World will abort the economic recovery in the industrial world. And a delayed recovery in the industrial world will visit even greater havoc on the stricken economies of the developing nations, and hence on the international financial system'.

The two most heavily-indebted nations, Brazil and Mexico, have already been forced to 'renegotiate their renegotiations' and it is estimated that neither country will be able to meet its debt service obligations in 1983 without more foreign borrowing. The *Financial Times* reported in May 1983: 'Brazil's obligations this quarter and next still far outweigh the inflows of hard currency when calculated on a cash basis'. *The Economist* has also stated: 'probably not later than October, Mexico is likely to have to go back to its bankers, its IMF targets missed, to beg another US$2 billion in emergency credits to see it through the year'.

Finally, the austerity programme imposed on Brazil by the IMF has already provoked a violent reaction from sectors of the Brazilian population. *The International Herald Tribune* commented: 'The rioting in São Paulo is an early warning of what can go wrong when austerity is imposed on an already hard-pressed population'. David Rockefeller, the retired chairman of Chase Manhattan Bank added: 'The problems ahead will be the political and social repercussions of the austerity measures those countries were forced to take to renew their credit'. If LDC governments were to be confronted by a militant population that will not accept the imposition of more austerity measures, and by international creditors who will not lend without such austerity programmes, then some governments may, in the words of Donald Regan, the US Treasury Secretary, 'be driven to consider other measures that could lead to widespread banking closures'.

According to UNCTAD, the emergency rescue operations mounted by the IMF over the past few months have done nothing more than push the crisis into the future. They argue that any plans negotiated without the participation of the LDCs will not produce the changes necessary to avoid recurrent crises. At the same time, any negotiations that do include the LDCs will result in demands for far more profound changes to the IMF and the international financial system than those now on offer.

Fundamental Reform

The need for fundamental reform of the IMF and the international financial system implies both rejection of the view that market forces can guarantee economic progress and of the belief that limited adjustments to market forces which the Fund is now undertaking will be sufficient to make any meaningful difference to the plight of the LDCs.

The reforms outlined in this section range from the views put forward by the two reports of the Brandt Commission, (*North-South: A Programme for Survival,* 1980; and *Common Crisis, North-South: Co-operation for World Recovery,* 1983) and views expressed by many LDCs in such forums as the Group of 77 and UNCTAD, to the proposals that emanated from the South-North Conference on the International Monetary System and the New International Order held in Arusha, Tanzania, in 1980. Underlying the range of views is the idea of mutuality of interests — i.e. that the proposed changes will be in the interests of both the developed countries and the LDCs.

The adjustment process and conditionality

While the IMF has been rigorous in its enforcement of balance of payments adjustment programmes for those countries suffering from balance of payments deficits, it has never seriously attempted to force adjustment on those countries with balance of payments surpluses. As every payments deficit must be counter-balanced somewhere in the world by a payments surplus, pressure on surplus countries to expand their economies, and thus increase their imports, would lead to decreases in the deficits of those countries exporting to the surplus nations. The IMF does have a 'scarce currency clause' which allows deficit countries to discriminate against the imports of surplus countries, thus pressing them to reduce their surpluses. However, that clause is virtually unenforceable as it stands at present. Those seeking substantial reform of the IMF recommend that surplus countries be made to play their part in the adjustment and not be left free, in the words of the Arusha Initiative, to 'solve their own short-term problems by exporting deflation and unemployment, and even to adopt protectionist measures against Third World imports'.

Another aspect of the adjustment involves the conditionality that the IMF brings to bear on deficit nations. The second Brandt Commission Report (Brandt II) suggests: 'The IMF, in framing its programmes, (should) give greater weight to output, growth employment and income distribution considerations, relative to its past emphasis on the control of inflation and demand management'. It suggests that the 1979 IMF guidelines — which stipulate that adjustment programmes pay 'due regard to the domestic, social and political objectives of the member countries' — should be implemented, thus making the conditionality attached to each adjustment process more appropriate to the situation of the borrower.

Furthermore, it is recognised that most LDCs avoid approaching the IMF for assistance because of the harsh conditions they know will be imposed. Thus, by the time they are *forced* to seek IMF help, their deficits are extreme, entailing drastic impositions by the Fund. Changes in conditionality, plus the increased resources that it is proposed the Fund should acquire, could persuade deficit countries to make much earlier use of the IMF, and allow for more 'understanding conditions' to be applied. This could, according to Brandt, reduce the IMF's 'ogrish reputation'.

Two areas where conditionality could be more flexible are, first, in the timing of adjustments and, second, in relation to deficits that are externally generated. The Fund should, it is suggested, be more realistic about the time it takes to make those adjustments that are needed to overcome the structural causes of balance of payments deficits. In this case the Extended Fund Facility, which funds long-term adjustments (e.g. the development of new industries or new markets to succeed old markets that may have been lost) and allows up to 10 years for repayment, should be increased to allow for more comprehensive structural adjustments.

Countries that face payments deficits for reasons beyond their own control, are badly served at present by IMF conditionality. A country whose deficit is caused by falling prices of its main export will not necessarily increase its export revenue, after the IMF has imposed a deflation to reduce prices, because world demand for those exports may still be crumbling. Brandt II's solution to this dilemma is to call for a 300 per cent increase in the Fund's Compensatory Finance Facility, which would compensate fully for that loss of export earnings caused by factors beyond the country's control. It also recommends that this facility should not be allocated on the basis of quotas. The quota system gives the poorest countries, those reliant on one or a few commodity exports and therefore with the greatest need for this type of compensation, least access to the resource. Rather, it should be allocated according to how severe a country's loss of export income has been.

Last, the reformers argue that the performance tests applied to ensure that a country is fully implementing the required conditions should be made more flexible and take account of a wider range of variables.

At present, the IMF uses conditionality as a way to force countries to adopt the IMF model of development. According to many LDCs, this interferes with a nation's sovereign right to decide its own social and economic models and development paths. The Arusha Initiative demands: 'There must be no penalization of countries which opt for strategies which emphasise national planning, systems of administrative budgeting (of foreign exchange, imports, investment and credit) that reform the traditional institutions, and an active role for the public sector'. Thus, the IMF would be obliged to provide finance to countries adopting models of development quite distinct to those suggested by the Fund's economists.

Increased resources for the IMF

In order for the adjustment described above to be successful, a much larger pool of resources must be made available to the IMF. Both the Brandt Report and the Group of 24 recommend that IMF quotas be increased by 100 per cent, which would enable the Fund to collect an extra US$45 million on top of the proposed 50 per cent quota increases already agreed. This very large increase is justified on the grounds that the value of IMF resources, as a percentage of world trade, has fallen from 12.3 per cent in 1960 to 3.2 per cent in 1981. Also, if the changes in conditionality outlined above were to be implemented, LDCs would be encouraged to call upon IMF resources more often and heavily. A very large quota increase would be needed to meet this extra demand. To supplement the extra quotas, the IMF should also, it is suggested, further increase the General Agreement to Borrow and begin to borrow from both central banks and the international money markets (effectively borrowing from the private banks). This would give the Fund the possibility of rapid expansion (or contraction) of its resources as circumstances changed. Besides, the Fund's resources should be augmented by a new issue of SDRs. Brandt II suggests US$10 billion to US$12 billion SDRs a year should be allocated for the next three years, if the proportion of SDRs to total IMF resources (other than gold) is to be restored to the ratio that existed in 1972.

The increase in IMF resources should not occur in a vacuum. The World Bank should lend more of its funds for long-term Structural Adjustment Loans (SALs) and its concessionary lending arm, the International Development Agency (IDA), should be substantially expanded. The developed countries could increase bilateral aid in accordance with the target of 0.7 per cent of a donor country's gross national product (agreed by the United Nations), with 0.5 per cent going to the poorest LDCs. The most controversial proposal might be the one that would have resources transferred automatically, rather than leaving the transfer to the whims of governments in donor countries. Therefore, some form of international tax (on the arms trade, for example) should be imposed so as to generate a constant stream of resources for LDCs.

International money, liquidity and a World Central Bank

The most fundamental reform of the IMF to have been put forward concerns the role SDRs should play in the international economy. As has already been outlined, the supply of 'world money' (those currencies used as international reserves and for international transactions) is crucial in the management of the world economy. At the moment, that supply is determined by the economic policy of the US and a few other Western nations. Yet that policy may not be in the interests of overall world trade. As the Bank for International Settlements has stated, the contraction of international liquidity in the 1980s is one of the 'factors which could impede the orderly resumption of economic growth or depress the world economy'. Therefore, it is suggested that SDRs should become the main form of international liquidity and be given the role of determining the overall increase in global liquidity. They should displace the dollar, gold and other currencies, and the level of their supply should be decided democratically by a representative World Central Bank.

Not only should the SDRs be the main form of international money, but their valuation should not depend on the values of the currencies of strong countries. At the moment, SDRs are valued according to the value of a basket of strong world currencies. This means that their values can be changed by the concerted action of a group of rich Western nations. An alternative suggestion is to value SDRs according to the value of a basket of internationally traded commodities, the value of which cannot be easily manipulated in the interest of any country or group of countries. Although there is no agreement as to the technical feasibility of this scheme, it is agreed that SDRs need a different method of valuation than the one at present operating, if they are to be an effective and independent world currency and resolve the problem of exchange rate instability.

Finally, SDRs should be allocated to those countries whose need is greatest, that is, those which have to finance the greatest balance of payments deficits and the most investment in economic adjustment programmes. At present, SDRs are allocated according to IMF quotas, thus ensuring that the powerful countries receive the largest allocation and the LDCs receive very little. The 'SDR link' would require that the allocation of SDRs be linked to the development needs of nations.

Democracy in the IMF

In order to implement the reforms outlined above, LDCs would need a much stronger voice in IMF decision-making. Therefore, the relative voting strength of all member countries would have to be revised so that one country, the US, did not have an effective veto and so that LDCs received more voting strength relative to the Group of Five nations. Also, in recognition of the power exercised by the IMF general manager and his staff, it is recommended that far more IMF staff should be appointed from the LDCs. Last, because differences of opinion between the IMF and debtor nations will always occur, it is recommended that an independent arbitration body, incorporating representatives of all parties, be set up and that its decisions be binding.

Assessment

Two types of proposal can be identified from the above recommendations. The first seeks to provide LDCs with more finance in order to proceed with their present model of development, and the second would allow LDCs more scope in determining other models of development that might better meet their needs.

Those reforms that recommend massive new lending (from various sources) to the deficit LDCs, but only minimal changes in the conditions attached to that lending, could lead to some growth in LDCs in the context of a growing world economy. However, as we have pointed out, such growth would be bought at the cost of further maladministration of the countries' resources in the hands of a small elite. Added to the bill would be increasing unemployment due to competition for local producers able to use only low-level technology, from transnational corporations with advanced technology to hand. Further, that source of growth reinforces a model of development that cannot lead to the integral development of an economy geared to meet the needs of the local population, but rather those of the international market.

Besides, and more importantly, such reforms could not bring about sustained growth. More lending may generate net inflows of capital into deficit LDCs in the short run, but they inevitably mean net outflows of capital in the long run. As *The Economist* has stated, 'the debt is a black hole, growing larger on the money it absorbs'. Thus, rather than providing the large and continuing inflows of capital for investment in the factories, roads and social services that the development process implies, increased borrowing serves only to pay off present debts at the expense of accumulating more future debts. According to the World Bank, 85 per cent of the new loans contracted by the LDCs in 1980 were used to repay old loans and therefore did not constitute a net inflow of capital into the LDCs concerned. Yet from 1978 to 1980, debt servicing, representing massive outflows of capital from the LDCs increased at an annual rate of 23.3 per cent.

It is not only the acquisition of debt capital that leads to the progressive decapitalization of LDCs. The current model of development that most LDCs adopt requires them to look to foreign transnational producers to provide the productive investment that the country needs to boost its output (and its exports, so it hopes) and to provide jobs. According to a report presented in Havana to the Conference of Non-Aligned Nations, foreign investments in LDCs from 1970 to 1978 have earned for their investors a return of no less than 237 per cent in profits, interests and royalties. That means an outflow from LDCs of US$2.3 million for every US$1 million that flows in.

It is difficult to see, therefore, how proposals for increased lending will resolve LDC problems in anything but the immediate future. The more radical proposals presented, massive automatic transfer of resources, a world currency not controlled by a handful of Western nations, changes of voting power within the IMF and an agreement that the Fund should not interfere if countries choose alternative development models, could make important changes in the world economy. The problem, however, is the likelihood of such changes ever being implemented.

There is a fundamental conflict of interest between the vast majority of people living in the LDCs and the powerful elites which control the rich Western nations. If the IMF is viewed as one of the instruments that these elites use to maintain their influence and control over the LDCs, there appears to be no reason why those who control the IMF should agree to changes that would be clearly against their own interests. Without the power necessary to force Western nations to accept such radical reforms, they will fall as nothing more than pious supplications on deaf ears.

Statistical Appendix

Notes to Statistical Appendix

The following tables are intended to give a selection and not a comprehensive survey, of data on the background to Latin American debt and to the IMF's operations in Latin America.

Argentina, Brazil and Mexico are listed separately in Tables 1, 2, 3, 4A-4D and 7 to take account both of the size of their economies and of the greater threat they pose to the world banking system by their combined debts.

The central problem with any debt tables is to define what is included in the debt. Different figures are reached according to different definitions of debt, which can include any of the following:

- *Undisbursed Debt:* the amount not yet drawn by the borrower from the creditor.
- *Public Debt:* the amount owed by a public debtor, including the national government, a political sub-division, a central bank or autonomous public bodies.
- *Publicly Guaranteed Debt:* the amount owed by a private debtor that is guaranteed by a public entity.
- *Private Non-guaranteed Debt:* the amount owed by a private debtor that is not guaranteed by a public entity.
- *Short-term Debt:* either defined as debt with an original maturity of less than one year, or any debt (of longer than one year maturity) that is due to be repaid within one year. This can include trade credit. The tables contain notes detailing which of the above are, included in each set of figures.

The four tables of debt indicators (4A-4D) are included to give an historical perspective on the evolution of the debts, and not to assess the capacity of any country to pay its debt. Although debt indicators can give useful information about developments in debt servicing capacity, conclusions drawn from them will not be valid unless accompanied by other economic evaluation. It is to be stressed that, in tables 4A and 4B, the figures are based on public debt only.

The various categories of creditors lending to Latin American countries appear at the bottom of Table 5.

Table 7 is included to show the drawings by Latin American countries on IMF facilities and also to highlight the case studies of Chile, Jamaica and Peru.

Table 8 is intended to illustrate the dwindling IMF quotas as a percentage both of LDC debt and world trade.

In accordance with conventional practice:
— indicates zero; n.a. indicates that the information is not available.

Table 1

STATISTICAL PROFILE 1981

	(1) Population (1980 — thousands)	(2) GNP (US$m)	(3) GNP (per capita) (US$m)	(4) Exports (US$m)	(5) Imports (US$m)	(6) Reserves (US$m)
Argentina	27,660	152,154*	5,500	11,788	15,757	5,006
Brazil	118,579	274,214	2,313	26,993	38,920	7,480
Mexico	69,900	230,724	3,301	30,083	43,222	4,971
Sub-total	**216,139**	**657,092**	**—**	**68,864**	**97,999**	**17,457**
Per cent of total	**63%**	**74%**	**—**	**56%**	**65%**	**36%**
Bahamas	224	727	3,246	1,154	1,243	100
Barbados	252	823	3,266	572*	620*	109
Bolivia	5,600	7,600	1,357	1,034	1,351	429
Chile	10,955	31,437	2,870	6,110	11,022	3,890
Colombia	26,173	36,319	1,388	4,953	6,888	6,079
Costa Rica	2,218	2,426	1,094	1,246	1,647	143
Dominican Republic	5,515	7,722	1,400	1,479*	2,171*	2,812

Ecuador	7,996	12,594	1,580	3,000	4,026	797
El Salvador	4,813	3,434	713	1,175*	1,302*	277
Guatemala	6,999	8,569	1,220	1,524	2,196	357
Guyana	787	561	710	411*	538*	7
Haiti	5,008	1,573	314	372	582	31
Honduras	3,703	2,598	700	903	1,233	107
Jamaica	2,174	2,676	1,231	1,562	1,961	85
Nicaragua	2,422	2,553	1,050	n.a.	n.a.	n.a.
Panama	1,895	3,670	1,937	4,282	4,640	120
Paraguay	3,168	5,109	1,613	694*	979*	820
Peru	16,678	20,906	1,250	4,217	5,902	1,764
Trinidad and Tobago	1,067	6,252	5,859	3,415*	4,117*	3,366
Uruguay	2,895	10,791	3,727	1,594*	2,312*	2,377*
Venezuela	13,943	67,047	4,809	24,484	20.440	12,719
Total	**340,624**	**892,479**	**—**	**122,375**	**151,418**	**48,932**

Sources: (1) IDB Annual Report 1982;
(2), (4), (5), (6) World Debt Tables 1982/3;
(3) = (2)/(1).
* 1980

123

Table 2

TOTAL DEBT 1960-1981[1] (US$ million)

	1960	1970	1972	1974	1976	1977	1978	1979	1980	1981
Argentina	1,275	2,455	3,448+	4,914+	6,519+	7,531+	12.045	16,380	19,093	26,705
Brazil	2,407	4,698	12,327	22,150	35,236	42,719	55,869	62,758	68,172	77,919
Mexico	1,151	3,792	4,754+	10,512+	18,291+	25,149+	30,970+	36,398+	38,910+	47,519
Sub-total	**4,833**	**10,945**	**20,529**	**37,576**	**60,046**	**75,399**	**98,884**	**115,536**	**126,175**	**152,143**
Per cent of Total	**67%**	**53%**	**59%**	**64%**	**67%**	**67%**	**69%**	**68%**	**67%**	**68%**
Bahamas	n.a.	50	48+	107+	100+	111+	99+	87+	80+	228+
Barbados	n.a.	16	12+	42+	72+	90+	112+	133+	161+	304+
Bolivia	179	551	744+	906+	1,608+	2,014+	2,371+	2,764+	2,944+	3,010+
Chile	562	2,534	3,598	4,956	5,062	5,623	7,183	8,273	9,780	13,075
Colombia	377	1,850	2,765	3,085	3,760	4,076	4,648	5,705	7,028	8,532
Costa Rica	55	227	297+	488+	1,002+	1,295+	1,622+	1,924+	2,480+	2.620+
Dominican Republic	6	290	336+	585+	784+	1,141	1,231	1,692	2,041	2,069
Ecuador	95	353	481+	604+	1,073+	1,790+	2,263+	2,948+	3,680+	4,257+
El Salvador	33	126	157+	296+	451+	451+	647+	717+	926+	1,034+
Guatemala	51	176	183+	200+	551+	658+	784+	837+	882+	1,041+

Guyana	50	123	224+	348+	457+	483+	656+	714+	743+	853+
Haiti	38	45	51+	85+	173+	212+	268+	348+	382+	464+
Honduras	23	144	169+	276+	704	951	1,134	1,419	1,901	2,103
Jamaica	n.a.	192	370+	714+	1,059+	1,179+	1,389+	1,498+	1.634+	1,809+
Nicaragua	41	222	332+	662+	964+	1.109+	1.207+	1,425+	2,108+	2,484+
Panama	59	290	467+	760+	1,435+	1,833+	2,363+	2,559+	2,836+	2,923+
Paraguay	22	158	193+	344	507	604	833	1,291	1,348	1,571
Peru	265	1,092	1,546+	3,435+	5,559+	6,438+	6,750+	7,997+	8,388+	8,468+
Trinidad and Tobago	21	122	149+	223+	157+	292+	527+	768+	757+	794+
Uruguay	132	356	402+	854	1,210	1,253	1,277	1,560	1,798	2,205
Venezuela	363	924	1,795+	1,890+	3,204+	4,781+	7,384+	10,239+	11,150+	11,535+
Total	**7,205**	**20,786**	**34,848**	**58,436**	**89,938**	**111,783**	**143,632**	**170,434**	**189,222**	**223,522**

Sources: IDB Annual Report 1982 for years 1960 and 1970.   World Debt Tables 1982/3 for years 1972-1981.

1. Total Debt includes all external debt, public or publicly guaranteed, with an original or extended maturity of more than one year, which is owed to non-residents and repayable in foreign currency, goods or services. Figures marked + include the debt of the private sector that is not guaranteed for repayment by a public entity. No figures include obligations with an original maturity of less than one year, debt repayable in local currency or most transactions with the IMF.

Table 3

TOTAL DEBT AND DEBT CHARACTERISTICS 1982[+]

	(1) Total Debt Year-end 1982 (US$bn)	(2) Short-term Year-end 1982 (US$bn)	(3) (2) as a per cent of (1)	(4) Owed to Commercial Banks (US$bn)	(5) Owed to US Banks (US$bn)	(6) (4) as a per cent of (1)
Argentina	38.5	19.0	49	25.3	8.8	66
Brazil	84.0	19.0	23	55.3	20.5	66
Mexico	80.0	31.0	39	64.4	25.2	81
Total	**202.5**	**69.0**	**34**	**145.0**	**54.5**	**72**
Per cent of Total	68%	66%	—	71%	67%	—
Bolivia	3.0	0.8	27	1.1	0.4	37
Chile	17.0	5.0	29	11.8	6.1	69
Colombia	10.3	4.0	39	5.5	3.0	53
Costa Rica	3.5	0.8	23	1.2	0.5	34
Ecuador	6.5	2.5	38	4.7	2.2	72
El Salvador	1.5	0.3	20	0.3	0.1	20
Guatemala	1.5	0.4	27	n.a.	0.2	n.a.
Honduras	2.0	0.4	20	0.5	0.3	25
Nicaragua	2.5	0.4	16	0.8	0.4	32
Paraguay	1.5	0.4	27	0.6	0.3	40
Peru	11.0	4.8	44	5.2	2.3	47
Uruguay	3.5	n.a.	n.a.	1.1	0.6	31
Venezuela	28.5	15.0	53	27.2	10.7	95
Total	**294.8**	**103.8**	**35**	**205.0**	**81.6**	**69**

Sources: (1), (2) and (5), *New York Times*, 13 March 1983 (Quoting Morgan Guaranty Trust).
(4) Morgan Guaranty Trust, *World Financial Markets*, February 1983.

+ Total Debt includes public and publicly guaranteed debt, and private non-guaranteed debt. Short-term debt is the debt due to be paid within one year.

126

Table 4A
TOTAL DEBT SERVICE AS A PERCENTAGE OF GNP 1972-1981[+]

	1972	1974	1976	1977	1978	1979	1980	1981
Argentina	1.9	1.4	1.6	2.1	3.3	1.4	1.3	n.a.
Brazil	1.0	1.1	1.3	1.6	2.2	2.9	3.3	3.1
Mexico	1.9	1.7	2.6	4.4	6.2	7.6	4.3	3.7
Bahamas	1.7	2.1	3.2	7.3	3.2	4.0	3.0	2.4
Barbados	3.5	1.3	0.9	1.9	1.6	2.0	1.6	1.8
Bolivia	3.1	3.2	3.6	4.7	8.9	5.3	4.7	3.7
Chile	0.8	2.6	7.9	6.8	8.1	6.3	5.2	5.3
Colombia	1.9	2.5	1.8	1.6	1.7	2.4	1.6	2.0
Costa Rica	2.8	3.2	2.9	2.9	7.0	6.5	4.4	7.2
Dominican Republic	0.8	1.1	1.4	1.6	1.9	4.6	2.3	3.0
Ecuador	2.1	2.7	1.6	1.8	2.8	8.0	3.8	4.3
El Salvador	0.9	1.5	1.6	2.5	1.0	1.0	1.2	1.3
Guatemala	2.0	0.9	0.3	0.3	0.5	0.6	0.8	0.6
Guyana	3.1	3.3	7.8	7.7	10.4	18.4	12.3	13.2
Haiti	0.8	0.9	1.2	1.2	1.2	0.7	1.1	1.3
Honduras	1.0	1.2	2.3	2.8	3.4	5.3	4.1	4.4
Jamaica	1.6	2.6	3.8	4.8	7.9	8.9	8.4	13.2
Nicaragua	3.8	3.5	4.3	5.0	5.2	3.8	3.7	1.4
Panama	4,1	7.6	5.2	7.7	23.5	14.0	14.3	13.4
Paraguay	1.9	1.3	1.2	1.3	1.4	1.6	1.8	1.4
Peru	2.2	3.4	3.2	4.9	6.7	6.4	8.2	9.1
Trinidad and Tobago	1.0	3.0	2.9	0.4	0.8	1.3	3.8	1.6
Uruguay	4.9	4.2	5.7	5.9	8.7	1.8	2.0	1.6
Venezuela	1.6	2.0	1.3	2.3	1.9	3.2	4.9	4.5
Average	**1.6**	**1.7**	**2.0**	**2.7**	**3.6**	**4.0**	**3.4**	**n.a.**

Source: World Debt Tables 1982/3.

+ Total Debt Service is the actual repayments of principal (amortisation) and interest made in foreign currencies, goods or services in the year specified. Total Debt Service is based on *public debt only*.

Table 4B

TOTAL DEBT SERVICE AS A PERCENTAGE OF EXPORTS 1972-1981[+]

	1972	1974	1976	1977	1978	1979	1980	1981
Argentina	20.5	16.8	18.5	15.4	27.0	14.7	17.7	18.2
Brazil	14.2	13.1	18.1	21.3	31.0	36.2	34.4	31.9
Mexico	22.3	18.8	31.1	43.3	54.6	62.3	31.8	28.2
Bahamas	n.a.	1.3	2.0	5.0	2.1	2.7	1.9	1.6
Barbados	5.7	2.0	1.9	3.7	2.8	3.0	2.3	n.a.
Bolivia	18.0	11.4	16.3	21.8	49.7	30.2	25.9	26.9
Chile	9.9	11.9	31.1	33.8	40.7	26.5	21.9	27.2
Colombia	12.5	15.8	9.5	8.8	9.4	13.3	9.7	14.6
Costa Rica	9.9	9.5	9.6	9.0	23.2	22.9	16.6	14.1
Dominican Republic	3.7	4.2	5.7	6.5	9.1	18.4	10.6	n.a.
Ecuador	10.5	7.1	5.7	7.3	12.0	29.5	13.7	17.9
El Salvador	3.1	4.6	4.0	6.0	2.8	2.2	3.5	n.a.
Guatemala	10.3	3.7	1.5	1.2	2.2	2.6	3.5	3.3
Guyana	5.2	4.5	11.2	11.7	15.8	28.7	16.8	n.a.
Haiti	4.5	5.4	4.7	4.9	4.0	2.7	3.9	5.4
Honduras	3.3	3.6	6.2	7.0	8.4	12.6	10.2	12.7
Jamaica	4.2	5.8	11.2	14.5	16.2	15.7	13.7	22.5
Nicaragua	11.1	11.3	12.1	13.9	13.6	8.1	n.a.	n.a.
Panama	10.5	12.8	8.2	11.6	32.5	18.4	12.5	11.5
Paraguay	13.4	7.8	7.7	6.3	7.2	8.9	11.5	n.a.
Peru	15.7	23.0	25.9	30.5	31.3	22.3	31.0	44.9
Trinidad and Tobago	2.5	4.7	5.6	1.0	1.9	2.4	6.5	n.a.
Uruguay	30.5	31.0	29.3	29.9	45.8	9.9	12.0	n.a.
Venezuela	6.2	4.2	3.9	7.6	6.9	9.5	13.3	12.5
Average	**13.6**	**11.3**	**15.2**	**18.3**	**26.2**	**26.6**	**22.2**	**n.a.**

Source: World Debt Tables 1982/3.

+ Total Debt Service is the actual repayments of principal (amortisation) and interest made in foreign currencies, goods or services in the year specified. Total Debt Service is based on *public debt only*.

Table 4C

RESERVES AS A PERCENTAGE OF TOTAL DEBT 1972-1981

	1972	1974	1976	1977	1978	1979	1980	1981
Argentina	17	38	30	51	49	71	49	19
Brazil	34	25	19	17	23	16	18	10
Mexico	27	18	8	8	7	8	11	10
Bahamas	n.a.	47	47	61	62	99	115	44
Barbados	233	93	39	41	54	50	49	33
Bolivia	10	28	13	15	13	19	19	14
Chile	5	6	12	12	20	33	42	30
Colombia	12	17	34	50	60	88	92	71
Costa Rica	15	11	10	16	13	8	8	5
Dominican Republic	18	18	17	17	14	17	14	14
Ecuador	30	65	49	38	32	32	34	19
El Salvador	61	57	56	65	59	56	41	27
Guatemala	81	137	101	114	109	115	85	34
Guyana	17	18	6	5	9	3	2	1
Haiti	35	24	16	17	15	9	7	7
Honduras	21	6	12	19	17	15	8	5
Jamaica	43	27	3	4	4	5	6	5
Nicaragua	24	16	15	14	5	n.a.	n.a.	n.a.
Panama	9	6	8	4	6	5	4	4
Paraguay	17	26	31	45	54	49	58	52
Peru	33	32	8	8	9	26	33	21
Trinidad and Tobago	39	175	646	509	344	282	371	424
Uruguay	74	87	54	72	87	128	132	n.a.
Venezuela	113	430	301	201	117	129	120	110
Average	**30**	**38**	**29**	**28**	**28**	**33**	**30**	**n.a.**

Source: World Debt Tables 1982/3 for international reserves and Table No.2 for total debt figures.

Table 4D

DEBT PER CAPITA: 1960, 1970, 1980, 1982

	1960	1970	1980	1982[1]
Argentina	62	106	690	1,392
Brazil	34	50	575	707
Mexico	33	78	557	1,144
Bahamas	n.a.	n.a.	357	n.a.
Barbados	n.a.	67	639	n.a.
Bolivia	54	112	526	536
Chile	73	270	893	1,552
Colombia	23	90	269	394
Costa Rica	44	133	1,118	1,578
Dominican Republic	2	72	370	n.a.
Ecuador	22	61	460	813
El Salvador	14	37	192	312
Guatemala	13	35	126	214
Guyana	87	165	944	n.a.
Haiti	11	11	76	n.a.
Honduras	12	59	513	540
Jamaica	n.a.	103	752	n.a.
Nicaragua	29	119	870	1,032
Panama	56	202	1,497	n.a.
Paraguay	13	71	426	473
Peru	26	81	503	660
Trinidad and Tobago	25	119	709	n.a.
Uruguay	53	133	621	1,209
Venezuela	49	90	800	2,044
Average	**36**	**79**	**555**	**911**

Sources: Table 2 and 3 for total debt figures. Population figures from IDB Annual Report 1982.

1. 1980 population figures used.

STRUCTURE OF LATIN AMERICAN DEBT, [+] BY TYPE OF CREDITOR, 1965-1980

| | PRIVATE | | | | OFFICIAL | | |
	Banks[1]	Suppliers[2]	Nationalisation[3] and Bond Issues[4]	Total per cent	Multi-lateral[5]	Bilateral[6]	Total per cent
1965	12.0	20.2	8.5	40.7	22.6	36.7	59.3
1970	19.5	16.9	8.3	44.7	24.4	30.9	55.3
1971	22.5	16.4	7.9	46.8	24.6	28.6	53.2
1972	26.2	14.7	7.3	48.2	24.2	27.6	51.8
1973	32.5	12.8	7.0	51.3	22.7	26.0	48.7
1974	37.7	12.0	6.0	55.7	20.0	24.3	44.3
1975	42.5	10.8	5.2	58.5	20.0	21.5	41.5
1976	46.7	9.0	5.8	61.5	18.6	19.9	38.5
1977	50.4	8.0	7.1	65.5	17.2	17.3	34.5
1978	53.4	7.2	7.8	68.4	16.3	15.3	31.6
1979	56.7	6.9	6.7	70.3	16.5	13.2	29.7
1980	56.1	6.2	7.4	69.7	17.3	13.0	30.3

Source: IDB Annual Report, 1982.

+ Debt repayable in foreign currency at more than one-year terms, contracted directly by public agencies or by private entities with government guarantee. Includes the undisbursed balance, but not private non-guaranteed debt.

Notes to Table 5

1. *Banks* comprises credits extended by commercial banks, whether their ownership is private or public, as well as credits from private financial institutions.
2. *Suppliers* includes credits from manufacturers, exporters or other suppliers of goods to finance the purchase of their products.
3. *Nationalisation* consists of debts which arise from the settlement for compensation to non-nationals for property owned by them, which has been acquired by the public authorities by means of expropriation or by common consent.
4. *Bond issues* comprises securities offered to the general public which are traded on stock exchanges, as well as securities privately placed with a limited number of investors, usually banking institutions, which could trade them on stock exchanges at a later date.
5. *Official multilateral* includes loans and credits extended by international, regional or sub-regional financial organisations, such as the World Bank, the International Development Association, the Inter-American Development Bank and the Central American Bank for Economic Integration. This category does not include loans made out of the funds administered by the IDB on behalf of governments.
6. *Official bilateral* includes direct loans from governments or public entities, and government loans administered by the IDB.

131

Table 6

LATIN AMERICA AND THE CARIBBEAN: AVERAGE TERMS OF PUBLIC DEBT, NEW COMMITMENTS 1972-1981

	1972	1974	1976	1977	1978	1979	1980	1981
All Creditors								
Interest (per cent)	6.9	9.2	7.5	8.0	9.4	11.2	11.6	14.2
Maturity period (years)	13.0	12.3	10.3	9.2	10.2	10.3	10.5	10.1
Grace period (years)	3.4	3.6	3.3	3.6	4.2	4.2	3.9	3.7
Official Creditors								
Interest (per cent)	6.0	6.1	6.7	7.0	6.8	6.9	7.4	8.3
Maturity period (years)	20.1	18.2	18.2	17.3	17.9	17.9	17.2	16.3
Grace period (years)	5.3	4.8	5.0	4.4	4.8	5.0	4.3	3.9
Private Creditors								
Interest (per cent)	7.5	10.5	7.8	8.2	10.0	12.1	13.3	15.9
Maturity period (years)	8.5	9.7	7.1	7.3	8.5	8.6	8.0	8.4
Grace period (years)	2.3	3.1	2.6	3.4	4.1	4.1	3.8	3.6

Source: World Debt Tables, 1982-3.

Table 7

USE OF IMF CREDITS (US$ million) 1972-1981[+]

	1972	1974	1976	1977	1978	1979	1980	1981
Argentina	189	78	529	419	—	—	—	—
Brazil	—	—	—	—	—	—	—	—
Mexico	—	—	371	509	299	136	—	—

Sub-Total	**189**	**78**	**900**	**928**	**299**	**136**	—	—
Bahamas	—	—	—	—	—	—	—	—
Barbados	9	—	—	8	9	9	3	1
Bolivia	86	18	—	—	20	20	80	71
Chile	—	196	467	365	347	179	123	49
Colombia	—	—	—	—	—	—	—	—
Costa Rica	4	23	38	36	32	58	57	103
Dominican Republic	9	—	25	44	48	124	49	23
Ecuador	10	22	15	—	—	—	—	—
El Salvador	—	—	—	—	—	—	7	44
Guatemala	—	—	—	—	—	—	—	111
Guyana	—	6	20	21	39	53	86	86
Haiti	—	8	14	10	10	8	22	37
Honduras	—	21	20	5	—	—	15	38
Jamaica	9	16	80	107	181	351	309	470
Nicaragua	—	12	10	2	3	57	49	25
Panama	—	9	50	51	53	42	23	94
Paraguay	33	—	—	—	—	—	—	—
Peru	—	—	184	205	334	492	474	387
Trinidad and Tobago	40	—	—	—	—	—	—	—
Uruguay	—	78	145	119	—	—	—	—
Venezuela	—	—	—	—	—	—	—	—
Total	**388**	**1,968**	**1,968**	**1,902**	**1,372**	**1,528**	**1,297**	**1,538**
Total (LDCs)	**1,159**	**2,678**	**7,356**	**7,158**	**7,182**	**7,778**	**9,075**	**13,680**
Latin American share (per cent) of LDC total	33	18	27	27	19	20	14	11

Source: World Debt Tables 1982/3.

+ All IMF resources except the reserve tranche and the IMF Trust Fund.

Table 8

IMF QUOTAS, VALUE OF WORLD IMPORTS AND TOTAL LDC DEBT

	(1) IMF quotas pre-1972: US$ million; post-1972; SDRs million	(2) Value of World Imports (US$bn)	(3) (1) as per cent of (2)	(4) Total LDC debt (US$bn)	(5) (1) as per cent of (4)
1947	7,922	39.5@ 56.4	20.1 14.0	n.a.	n.a.
1950	8,037	59.5	13.5	n.a.	n.a.
1955	8,751	88.3	9.9	n.a.	n.a.
1960	14,741	119.6	12.3	n.a.	n.a.
1965	15,972	174.2	9.2	38.1	42
1970	23,182	294.7	7.9	72.9	32
1972	28,988	385.1	8.8	90.7	32
1974	29,189	781.0	3.7	135.8	21
1975	29,211	814.4	3.6	161.9	18
1976	29,213	923.2	3.2	195.5	15
1977	29,219	1,059.0	2.8	240.1	12
1978	39,011	1,237.8	3.2	298.8	13
1979	39,015	1,559.5	2.5	352.4	11
1980	59,596	1,923.2	3.1	404.8	15
1981	60,674	1,907.8	3.2	462.1	13
1982	60,060	1,770.0[+] [a]	3.4	529.0[+] [b]	11
1983	90,000	n.a.	n.a.	706.0[+] [c]	13

Sources: International Financial Statistics (various years) for (1) and (2). World Debt Tables for (4).

@ Figure obtained from International Financial Statistics 1948. The figure below is obtained from *IFS* 1950.

+. estimate.   a. is from International Financial Statistics 1983.   b. is from World Debt Tables.   c. is from *Time Magazine,* 10 January 1983.

Suggested Reading

J.K. Horsefield, *The International Monetary Fund 1954-1965,* three volumes, IMF, Washington, 1969.

M.G. de Vries, *The International Monetary Fund, 1966-1971,* two volumes, IMF, Washington, 1976.

For current information from the IMF see *The IMF Survey* (bi-monthly) and *Finance and Development* (quarterly).

Tony Killick (ed), *Adjustment and Financing in the Developing World: The Role of the IMF,* IMF and Overseas Development Institute, London. 1982.

Developing Country Bank Debt: Crisis Management and Beyond, ODI Briefing Paper No.2, March 1983.

NACLA, *Public Debt and Private Profit,* Report on the Americas, Vol.XII, No.4, July-August, New York, 1978.

The Brandt Commission, *Common Crisis, North-South: Co-operation for World Recovery,* Pan Books, London, 1983.

The Brandt Commission, *North-South: A Programme for Survival,* Pan Books, London, 1980.

The Wilson Centre, *The Americas at a Crossroads,* Report of the Inter-American Dialogue, Washington, 1983.

Dag Hammarskjöld Foundation, *Development Dialogue No.2,* Uppsala, 1980.

N. Butler, *The IMF: Time for Reform,* Young Fabians, London, 1982.

Anthony Sampson, *The Money Lenders: Bankers in a Dangerous World,* Hodder and Stoughton, London, 1981.

S. Strange, *International Monetary Relations,* OUP, London, 1976.

C. Payer, *The Debt Trap,* Penguin, Harmondsworth, 1974.

Contemporary material concerning the IMF and the Debt Crisis can be found in the *Financial Times, The International Herald Tribune, The Economist, The Guardian, Time Magazine, The Banker* and *Euromoney.*

Chile

Robert Carty, *Miracle or Mirage? A Review of Chile's Economic Model 1973-1980,* Taskforce on the Churches and Corporate Responsibility, Toronto, 1982.

Laurence Whitehead, *Inflation and Stabilisation in Chile 1970-1977,* in Rosemary Thorpe and Laurence Whitehead (eds) *Inflation and Stabilisation in Latin America,* Macmillan Press, London, 1979.

Stephany Griffith-Jones, *International Financial Institutions and Their Impact on Chilean Economic Policy and Development between 1973 and 1978,* mimeo, 1981.

Peru

E.V.K. Fitzgerald, *The Political Economy of Peru, 1956-78,* Cambridge University Press, 1980.

R. Thorp and G. Bertram, *Peru 1890-1977, Growth and Policy in an Urban Economy,* Macmillan, 1978.

B. Stallings, *Peru and the US Banks, Privatisation of Financial Relations,* in R. Fagan (ed.) *Capitalisation and the State in US Latin America Relations,* Stanford University Press, 1978.

T. Pinzas Garcia, *La Economia Peruana, 1950-78, Ensayo Bibliográfico,* IEP Lima, 1981.

Latin America Perspectives, *Peru — Bourgeois Revolution and Class Struggle,* No.14, Vol.IV, No.3, Summer 1977.

Jamaica

N. Girvan and R. Bernal, *The IMF and the Foreclosure of Development Options: The Case of Jamaica.* Monthly Review, Vol.33, No.9, February 1982.

Winston James, *The Decline and Fall of Michael Manley: Jamaica 1972-1980.* Capital and Class, No.19, Spring 1983.

George Beckford and Michael Witter, *Small Garden . . . Bitter Weed: Struggle and Change in Jamaica.* Zed Press, London, 1982.

Fitzroy Ambursley, *Jamaica: The Demise of Democratic Socialism.* New Left Review, No.128, July-August 1981.

CHILE: The Pinochet Decade

Ten years ago, General Pinochet came to power in Chile in a coup which cost the lives of over 10,000 people. The coup brought to an end the socialist government of President Allende and inaugurated an experiment in monetarist economics which *Time Magazine* described as 'a model of what can be achieved in restructuring an ageing prostrate economy into a streamlined machine.' A decade later, the experiment has collapsed. Chile has entered the worst economic crisis in its history and Pinochet is facing widespread opposition.

Chile: The Pinochet Decade tells the story of the rise and fall of the *laissez-faire* ecnomic technocrats known as the Chicago Boys, who masterminded the experiment and analyses the nature of their alliance with General Pinochet. The book shows how the Chicago Boys promoted a concept of 'economic liberty' based on the individual's right to compete in free markets. This could only be implemented through a state with vastly increased powers of repression and surveillance. In this way, manual and white collar workers and the rural and urban poor were forced to accept dramatic falls in their living standards which were a consequence of the model. For, the Chicago Boys presupposed a political and economic system, in which only the privileged few are actors and notions of social justice do not figure.

Chile: The Pinochet Decade traces the failure of the model from the 'shock treatment' of 1975, in which the economy was massively contracted in order to reduce inflation, through the supposed miracle years of high growth funded by foreign loans, to the present situation of bankruptcy and the final abandonment of the free market model.

Latin America Bureau

Available from **Latin America Bureau, 1 Amwell Street, London EC1R 1UL**

£2.95 plus £0.75 postage and packing
US$6.00 plus US2.50 postage and packing
ISBN 0 906156 18 1   Published September 1983

BRAZIL
State and Struggle

Brazil has been under military rule since 1964. Since then there has been substantial repression, the growth of poverty, massive urban migration of the rural dispossessed, and a huge increase in foreign ownership of land and industry. Brazil owes the international bankers over eighty billion dollars and is groaning under an inflation rate of 100%. The so-called 'economic miracle' has been unmasked as a brief period of industrial expansion which occurred at huge social cost to the majority of Brazilians.

Brazil: State and Struggle traces the origins and development of the current crisis in Brazil from the 1920s to the present. It pays particular attention to the current phase in which the growth of an independent trade union movement has been the major feature. Under pressure from the emerging popular movement, the military and the industrialists have initiated a process of 'reform' or *abertura*. Yet these measures have proved to be very limited, and designed to sustain the dictatorship rather than to democratise Brazil.

LAB's Special Brief provides an up-to-date analysis of Latin America's most sizeable, most populated and most industrialised country.

Latin America Bureau

Available from **Latin America Bureau, 1 Amwell Street, London EC1R 1UL**

£2.50 plus £0.50 postage and packing
US$5.00 plus US$2.00 postage and packing
ISBN 0 906156 16 5   Published 1982